The Craftsman Series

THE
AUTOBIOGRAPHY OF
JAMES NASMYTH
ENGINEER

JAMES NASMYTH

From an etching by Paul Rajon after a portrait by George Reid, R.S.A.

The

AUTOBIOGRAPHY OF
JAMES NASMYTH

ENGINEER

PASSAGES SELECTED
TO FORM A CONTINUOUS NARRATIVE
FROM THE ORIGINAL EDITION OF
SAMUEL SMILES, LL.D.

Edited by

A. F. COLLINS, B.Sc.
Inspector of Handicraft and Science
Birmingham Education Authority

CAMBRIDGE
AT THE UNIVERSITY PRESS
1931

CAMBRIDGE UNIVERSITY PRESS
Cambridge, New York, Melbourne, Madrid, Cape Town,
Singapore, São Paulo, Delhi, Mexico City

Cambridge University Press
The Edinburgh Building, Cambridge CB2 8RU, UK

Published in the United States of America by Cambridge University Press, New York

www.cambridge.org
Information on this title: www.cambridge.org/9781107610910

First published 1931
First paperback edition 2013

A catalogue record for this publication is available from the British Library

ISBN 978-1-107-61091-0 Paperback

CONTENTS

ILLUSTRATIONS

PLATES

TEXT-FIGURES

EDITOR'S PREFACE

An examination of the literature suitable to the needs of adolescent readers and available for their use, especially in schools, brings to light the fact that it includes few books which reveal the personality of the craftsman as well as the interest of his work. Yet no reflective person can fail to realise how great a part the development of constructive activities in the sphere of material things has played in the progress of mankind.

That young people are interested in craftsmen and their work is clear from the popularity, particularly among boys, of books which describe the more spectacular achievements of the engineer and inventor. But such books are for the most part written more with the aim of presenting technicalities in a popular and readable form than of showing us the craftsman himself—the man behind the work. Moreover, their literary standard is often such that they are not usually regarded as subjects for other than purely recreative reading.

Records of their work written by practising craftsmen, or by those who, while directing the work of others, show an intimate knowledge of a craft gained only through an arduous apprenticeship, are not common. They do exist, however, and contain literature of real worth, full of human as well as of technical interest.

The object of "The Craftsman Series" is to make this literature available in a form convenient for school use, especially at the present time, when so much attention is being given to the practice of the crafts as a part of general education, and to the need for a suitable literary and historical background for more specialised technical studies.

The Editor's contribution to the present volume, apart from the work of selection and arrangement, consists of an introductory chapter, together with a few brief footnotes and linking-up passages, which are printed in italics to distinguish them from the Author's original notes.

Several of the illustrations here printed appeared in the first edition of the "Autobiography": these have been supplemented by others from the sources acknowledged below, with the result, it is hoped, of making this volume a more complete and attractive account of Nasmyth's technical achievements.

Any impartial historian of the Bridgewater Foundry—the engineering works begun by Nasmyth and still the home of the great Firm of which he was the founder—cannot fail to observe that the Author of the "Autobiography" makes no mention of his brother George Nasmyth, who was a partner with him during the first seven years of the Firm's existence.

Whatever may be the reason for this noteworthy omission, it in no wise detracts from the value and interest of the book as an authentic description of the work of one of the great figures in the history of mechanical engineering.

In compiling this volume from the much larger original "Autobiography", which was published in 1883, the Editor has sought to present a continuous narrative formed mainly of the passages relating to Nasmyth's development as a craftsman. From the schoolboy whose classical education (in a class of 200!) made little appeal to him, but who was famed among his fellows for his home-made spinning tops and toy cannon, to the active head of a great engineering concern, Nasmyth's work, and his thoughts upon his work, are full of interest, and amply justify the inclusion of the "Autobiography" in "The Craftsman Series".

The sincere thanks of the Editor are due to the following for assistance with, and permission to reproduce, certain of the illustrations in this volume: Mr John Murray; The Trustees of the British Museum; The Director and Secretary of the Science Museum, South Kensington; Messrs W. and T. Avery, Ltd., of Soho Foundry, Birmingham; and Messrs Nasmyth, Wilson and Co., Ltd., of the Bridgewater Foundry, Patricroft.

A. F. C.

BIRMINGHAM
March 1931

INTRODUCTION

MOST people know something of the great changes brought about in industry by the application of steam power. In the later years of the eighteenth century the work of James Watt and others changed the steam-engine from a clumsy and expensive contrivance, suited only for pumping water from mines, into a much less wasteful and more convenient mechanism, and made it possible for steam to be used as the driving force in the work of numberless factories.

But not every one realises that the increased use of steam power brought its difficulties and problems, as well as its advantages, to the craftsmen of the time. These difficulties lay in the fact that the inventors, who were hard at work improving the steam-engine, were making demands in advance of the craftsmanship of those days. To bring their inventions into practical form they needed things made, and made in quantity, which were then actually beyond the powers of the great majority of workmen.

Thus James Watt encountered astonishing trials in having his early engines constructed. Cylinders, upon the accuracy of which the efficient working of the engines depended, were so badly cast and bored that the steam leaked in all directions, and pistons could only be kept steam-tight by packing them with paper, cork, putty, cardboard, or old beaver hats! Watt frequently complained of "the villainous bad workmanship" of the time.

Other inventors had similar experiences. Joseph Bramah, best known as the inventor of the hydraulic press, in 1784 invented and patented a door-lock which was a vast improvement on any lock then known. Yet until he took Henry

Maudsley, afterwards the teacher of James Nasmyth, into his workshop he was almost in despair over the problem of producing his very delicate lock-mechanisms accurately and at such a speed as to be able to sell them for a reasonable price. The elder Brunel, who devised a complicated series of machines for making pulley-blocks for the Navy, in the year 1800 had the greatest difficulty in finding engineers capable of making them.

Why was this so? The need for extreme precision in metal-working was not felt until then, and hence there were few craftsmen ready to meet the demands of the inventors. William Fairbairn, himself a well-known engineer, once said that in 1814, when he started work in Manchester, "there were neither planing, slotting nor shaping machines, and with the exception of very imperfect lathes and a few drills, the operations of construction were carried on entirely by the hands of the work-men".[1]

The progress of invention called into existence a type of craftsman almost unknown until the nineteenth century—the skilled and accurate engineer, able to work to the most precise measurements. And to-day all kinds of mechanisms are made in metal, not only with the utmost exactness, but at a speed undreamed of a century ago.

James Nasmyth was one of the greatest of the men who have bridged this gap between the crude workmanship of the late eighteenth century and the astonishingly complicated and accurate automatic machinery so common in factories to-day.

The earliest of them had few mechanical devices to aid their skill of hand and eye. Laborious and amazingly accurate handwork was their only means of making machinery. Specimens of their craft preserved to-day fill us with admiration of the quality of their workmanship. But at what a cost of time and patient skill was it produced!

[1] *Address to the British Association, Manchester, 1861.*

These simple but really accurate machines, however, made it possible for other and more complicated mechanisms to be made, and so the process of improvement went on, until to-day we have the kind of thing shown in the picture facing p. 92—a modern machine shop which would not have been possible but for the work of these early engineers.

In this story of Nasmyth's life you will read of his youthful work as an amateur craftsman, and of his later training under Henry Maudsley, one of the most accurate and ingenious workers of his day. You will read how Nasmyth started in business on his own account with but one assistant, making his own machines to equip his simple workshop, and of how his business grew into the great Bridgewater Foundry, which to-day sends its locomotive engines to all parts of the world. You will read how he came to invent the steam hammer, in connection with which his name is best known.

But perhaps the most interesting feature of Nasmyth's "Autobiography" is not the story of the growth of his business, nor even that of his great invention, but rather the way in which he reveals to us the fascination which fine craftsmanship always had for him, and the respect in which he held all men who, in the craftsman's blunt phrase, "really knew their jobs".

CHAPTER I

The Family of Nasmyth

(The ancestors of James Nasmyth were the Naesmyths of Netherton, an old Scottish family who lost all their property in the Rebellion of the Covenanters, in the reign of Charles the Second.)

THE NAESMYTHS of Netherton, having lost their ancestral property, had to begin the world again. But they had plenty of pluck and energy. I go back to my great-great-grandfather, Michael Naesmyth, who was born in 1652. He occupied a house in the Grassmarket, Edinburgh, in 1696. His business was that of a builder and architect. His chief employment was in designing and erecting new mansions, principally for the landed gentry and nobility. Michael Naesmyth acquired a high reputation for the substantiality of his work. His masonry was excellent, as well as his woodwork.

The business was afterwards carried on by Michael's son, my great-grandfather. He was a man of much ability and of large experience. One of his great advantages in carrying on his business was the support of a staff of able and trustworthy foremen and workmen. The times were very different then from what they are now. Masters and men lived together in mutual harmony. There was a kind of loyal family attachment among them, which extended through many generations. Workmen had neither the desire nor the means for shifting about from place to place. On the contrary, they settled down with their wives and families in houses of their own, close to the workshops of their employers. Work was found for them in the dull seasons when trade was slack, and in summer they sometimes removed to jobs at a distance from headquarters.

My grandfather, Michael Naesmyth, succeeded to the business in 1751. He more than maintained the reputation of his predecessors.

I remember my father pointing out to me the extreme care and attention with which he finished his buildings. He inserted small fragments of basalt into the mortar of the external joints of the stones, at close and regular distances, in order to protect the mortar from the adverse action of the weather. And to this day they give proof of their efficiency; the basalt protects the joints, and at the same time gives a neat and pleasing effect to what would otherwise have been the merely monotonous line of mason-work.

My grandfather built the first house in the southwest corner of St Andrew Square (*Edinburgh*), for the occupation of David Hume the historian, as well as the two most important houses in the centre of the north side of the square. All these houses are still in perfect condition,[1] after resisting the ordinary tear and wear of upwards of a hundred and ten northern winters.

I must again refer to the highly finished character of my grandfather's work. Nothing merely moderate would do. The work must be of the very best. He took special pride in the sound quality of the woodwork and its careful workmanship. He chose the best Dantzic timber because of its being of purer grain and freer from knots than other wood. In those days the lower parts of the walls of the apartments were wainscoted— that is, covered by timber framed in large panels. They were from three to four feet wide, and from six to eight feet high. To fit these in properly required the most careful joiner-work.

It was always a holiday treat to my father, when a boy, to be permitted to go down to Leith to see the ships discharge their cargoes of timber. My grandfather had a wood-yard at Leith, where the timber selected by him was piled up to be seasoned

---

[1] *In 1881–2, when the "Autobiography" was written.*

and shrunk, before being worked into its appropriate uses. He was particularly careful in his selection of boards or strips for floors, which must be perfectly level, so as to avoid the destruction of the carpets placed over them. The hanging of his doors was a matter that he took great pride in—so as to prevent any uneasy action in opening or closing. His own chamber doors were so well hung that they were capable of being opened and closed by the slight puff of a hand-bellows.

The excellence of my grandfather's workmanship was a thing that my own father always impressed upon me when a boy. It stimulated in me the desire to aim at excellence in everything that I undertook; and in all practical matters to arrive at the highest degree of good workmanship. I believe that these early lessons had a great influence upon my future career.

My father, Alexander Nasmyth, was the second son of Michael Naesmyth.[1] He was born in his father's house in the Grassmarket on the 9th of September, 1758.

At a very early period my father exhibited a decided natural taste for art. He used his pencil freely in sketching from nature; and in course of time he showed equal skill in the use of oil colour. At his own earnest request he was bound apprentice to Mr Crighton, then the chief coach-builder in Edinburgh. He was employed in that special department where artistic taste was necessary—that is, in decorating the panels of the highest class of carriages, and painting upon them coats of arms, with their crests and supporters. He took great pleasure in this kind of work. It introduced him to the practical details of heraldry, and he made great progress in his business.

But at length an important change took place in his career. Allan Ramsay, son of the author of *The Gentle Shepherd*, and then court painter to George III, called upon his old friend Crighton one day, to look over his works. There he found young Nasmyth

[1] *At about this time the "e" was dropped from the family name.*

painting a coat of arms on the panel of a carriage. He was so much struck with the lad's artistic workmanship—for he was then only sixteen—that he formed a strong desire to take him into his service. After much persuasion, backed by the offer of a considerable sum of money, the coach-builder was at length induced to transfer my father's indentures to Allan Ramsay.

It was, of course, a great delight to my father to be removed to London under such favourable auspices. Ramsay had a large connection as a portrait painter. His object in employing my father was that the latter should assist him in the execution of the subordinate parts, or dress portions, of portraits of courtiers, or of diplomatic personages. No more favourable opportunity for advancement could have presented itself.

My father remained in Allan Ramsay's service until the end of 1778, when he returned to Edinburgh to practise on his own behalf the profession of portrait painter. During the first year of my father's married life, when he lived in St James' Square, he painted the well-known portrait of Robert Burns the poet.

Besides portrait painting, my father was much employed in assisting the noblemen and landed gentry of Scotland in improving the landscape appearance of their estates, especially when seen from their mansion windows. His fine taste and his love of natural scenery gave him great advantages in this respect. He selected the finest sites for the new mansions when they were erected in lieu of the old towers and crenellated castles.

He was greatly interested in the architectural beauty of his native city, and he was professionally consulted by the authorities about the laying out of the streets of the New Town. The subject occupied much of his time and thought, especially when resting from the mental fatigue arising from a long sitting at his easel. It was his regular practice to stroll about where the building work was in progress, or new roads were being laid out, and watch the proceedings with keen interest. This was probably due to the taste which he had inherited from his fore-bears—more especially from his father, who had begun the buildings of the New Town.

Then, with respect to my father's powers as a mechanic: this was an inherited faculty, and I leave my readers to infer from the following pages whether I have not had my fair share of this inheritance. Besides his painting room, my father had a workroom fitted up with all sorts of mechanical tools. It was one of his greatest pleasures to occupy himself there as a relief from sitting at his easel, or while within doors from the inclemency of the weather. The walls and shelves of his work-room were crowded with a multitude of artistic and ingenious mechanical objects, nearly all of which were the production of his own hands. His natural taste for order and arrangement gave it a very orderly aspect, however crowded its walls and shelves might be. Everything was in its place, and there was a place for everything. It was in this workroom that I first began to handle mechanical tools. It was my primary technical school —the very foreground of my life.

One of his inventions was the method of riveting by com-pression instead of by blows of the hammer. It originated in a slight circumstance. One wet, wintry Sunday morning he went into his workroom. There were some slight mechanical repairs to be performed upon a beautiful little stove of his own con-struction. To repair it, iron rivets were necessary to make it serviceable. But as the hammering of the hot rivets would annoy his neighbours by the unwelcome sound of the hammer, he solved the difficulty by using the jaws of his bench vice to *squeeze* the hot rivets in when put into their places. The stove was thus quickly repaired in the most perfect silence.

This was, perhaps, the first occasion on which a squeeze or compressive action was substituted for the percussive action of the hammer, in closing red-hot rivets, for combining together pieces of stout sheet or plate iron. This system of riveting was long afterwards patented by Smith of Deanston in combination with William Fairbairn of Manchester; and it was employed in riveting the plates used in the construction of the bridges over the River Conway and the Menai Strait.

It is also used in boiler and girder making, and in other wrought-iron structures in which thoroughly sound riveting is absolutely essential; and by the employment of hydraulic power in a portable form a considerable portion of iron shipbuilding is effected by the silent *squeeze* system in place of hammers, much to the advantage of the soundness of the work. My father frequently, in after-times, practised this mode of riveting by compression in place of using the blow of a hammer; and in remembrance of the special circumstances under which he contrived this silent and most effective method of riveting, he named it 'The Sunday Rivet'.

CHAPTER II

My Early Life and School-days

I WAS born on the morning of the 19th of August, 1808, at my father's house, No. 47 York Place, Edinburgh. I was named James Hall after my father's dear friend, Sir James Hall of Dunglass. When I was about four or five years old, I was observed to give a decided preference to the use of my left hand. Everything was done to prevent my using it in preference to the right. My mother thought that it arose from my being carried on the wrong arm by my nurse while an infant. The right hand was thus confined, and the left hand was used. I was constantly corrected, but 'on the sly' I always used it, especially in drawing

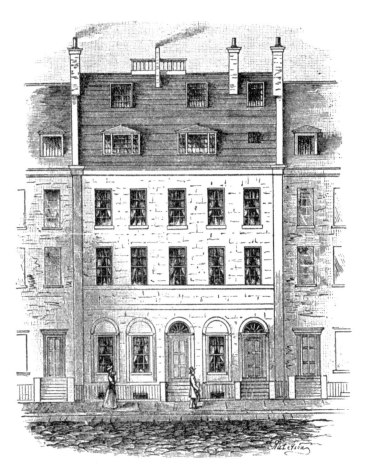

No. 47 York Place, Edinburgh
The Birthplace of James Nasmyth

my first little sketches. At last my father, after viewing with
pleasure one of my artistic efforts, done with the forbidden hand,
granted it liberty and independence for all time coming. 'Well,'
he said, 'you may go on in your own way in the use of your left
hand, but I fear you will be an awkward fellow in everything
that requires handiness in life.' I used my right hand in all that
was necessary, and my left in all sorts of practical manipulative
affairs. My left hand has accordingly been my most willing
and obedient servant in transmitting my will through my
fingers into material or visible forms. In this way I became
ambidexter.

I am reminded, by reading over a letter of my brother
Patrick's, of an awkward circumstance which happened to me
when I was six years old. In his letter to my father, dated
London, 22nd September 1814, he says: 'I did get a surprise
when Margaret's letter informed me of my little brother Jamie's
fall. It was a wonderful escape. For God's sake keep an eye
upon him!' Like other strong and healthy boys, I had a turn
for amusing myself in my own way. When sliding down the
railing of the stairs I lost my grip and fell suddenly off. The
steps were of stone. Fortunately, the servants were just coming
in laden with carpets which they had been beating. I fell into
their midst and knocked them out of their hands. I was thus
saved from cracking my poor little skull. But for that there
might have been no steam-hammer—at least of my contrivance!

One of my greatest enjoyments when a child was in going out
with the servants to the Calton, and waiting while the 'claes'
bleached in the sun on the grassy slopes of the hill. The air was
bright and fresh and pure. The lasses regarded these occasions
as a sort of holiday. One or two of the children usually accompanied them. The women brought their work and their needles
with them, and when they had told their stories, the children
ran about the hill, making bunches of wild flowers. They ran

after the butterflies and the 'bumbees', and made acquaintance in a small way with the beauties of nature. Then the servants opened their baskets of provisions, and we had a delightful picnic. Though I am now writing about seventy years after the date of these events, I can almost believe that I am enjoying the delightful perfume of the wild thyme and the fragrant plants and flowers, wafted around me by the warm breezes of the Calton hillside.

While enjoying these delightful holidays, before my school-days began, my practical education was in progress, especially in the way of acquaintance with the habits of nature in a vast variety of its phases, always so attractive to the minds of healthy children. It happened that close to the Calton Hill, in the valley at its northern side, there were many workshops where interesting trades were carried on, such as those of coppersmiths, tinsmiths, brassfounders, goldbeaters, and blacksmiths. Their shops were all gathered together in a busy group at the foot of the hill, in a place called Greenside. The workshops were open to the inspection of passers-by. Little boys looked in and saw the men at work amidst the blaze of fires and the beating of hammers.

Amongst others, I was an ardent admirer. I may almost say that this row of busy workshops was my first school of practical education. I observed the mechanical manipulation of the men, their dexterous use of the hammer, the chisel, and the file; and I imbibed many lessons which proved of use to me in my later years. Then I had tools at home in my father's workshop. I tried to follow their methods; I became greatly interested in the use of tools and their appliances; I could make things for myself. In short, I became so skilled that the people about the house called me 'a little Jack-of-all-trades'.

Before I went to school it was my good fortune to be placed under the special care of my eldest sister, Jane. I could not have had a more careful teacher. She initiated me into the depths of the ABC, and by teaching me to read she gave me the key to the greatest thoughts of the greatest thinkers who have ever lived.

But all this was accomplished at first in a humdrum and tentative way. About seventy years ago children's books were very uninteresting. In the little stories manufactured for children, the good boy ended in a coach-and-four, and the bad boy in a ride to Tyburn. The good boys must have been a set of little snobs and prigs, and I could scarcely imagine that they could ever have lived as they were represented in these goody books. If so, they must have been the most tiresome and uninteresting vermin that can possibly be imagined.

I was entered as a pupil at the Edinburgh High School in October 1817. I was set to study Latin under Mr Irvine. He was a mere schoolmaster in the narrowest sense of the term. He was not endowed with the best of tempers, and it was often put to the breaking strain by the tricks and negligence of the lower form portion of his class. It consisted of nearly two hundred boys; the other three masters had about the same number of scholars. They each had a separate class-room.

I began to learn the elementary rudiments of Latin grammar. But not having any natural aptitude for acquiring classic learning so called, I fear I made but little progress during the three years that I remained at the High School. Had the master explained to us how nearly allied many of the Latin and Greek roots are to our familiar English words, I feel assured that so interesting and valuable a department of instruction would not have been neglected. But our memories were strained by being made to say 'off by heart', as it was absurdly called, whole batches of grammatical rules, with all the botheration of irregular verbs and such like. So far as I was concerned I derived little benefit from my High School teaching, except that I learned one lesson which was of great use in after life. I mean as regards the performance of duty. I did my tasks punctually and cheerfully, though they were far from agreeable. This is an exercise in early life that is very useful in later years.

Like many serious-minded boys, I had a severe attack at the right time of life, say from 12 to 15, of what I would call 'the collecting period'. This consisted, in my case, of accumulating old coins, perhaps one of the most salutary forms of this youthful passion. I made exchanges with my school companions. Sometimes my father's friends, seeing my anxiety to improve my collection, gave me choice specimens of bronze and other coins of the Roman emperors, usually duplicates from their own collections. These coins had the effect of promoting my knowledge of Roman history. I read up in order to find out the acts and deeds of the old rulers of the civilised world. Besides collecting the coins, I used to make careful drawings of the obverse and reverse faces of each in an illustrated catalogue which I kept in my little coin cabinet.

I did not long continue my passion for the collection of coins. I felt a greater interest in mechanical pursuits. I have a most cherished and grateful remembrance of the happy hours and days that I spent in my father's workroom. When the weather was ungenial he took refuge amongst his lathes and tools, and there I followed and watched him. He took the greatest pleasure in instructing me. Even in the most humble mechanical job he was sure to direct my attention to the action of the tools and to the construction of the work he had in hand, and to point out the manipulative processes requisite for its being effectually carried out. My hearty zeal in assisting him was well rewarded by his implanting in my mind the great fundamental principles on which the practice of engineering in its grandest forms is based. But I did not learn all this at once. It only came gradually, and by dint of constant repetition and inculcation. In the meantime I made a beginning by doing some little mechanical work on my own account.

While attending the High School, from 1817 to 1820, there was the usual rage amongst boys for spinning-tops, 'peeries', and 'young cannon'. By means of my father's excellent foot-lathe I turned out the spinning-tops in capital style, so much so that I became quite noted amongst my school companions. They all wanted to have specimens of my productions. They would give any price for them. The peeries were turned with perfect accuracy, and the steel shoe, or spinning pivot, was centred so as to correspond with the heaviest diameter at the top. They would spin twice as long as the bought peeries. When at full speed they would 'sleep', that is, turn round without a particle of waving. This was considered high art as regarded top-spinning.

Flying-kites and tissue paper balloons were articles that I was somewhat famed for producing. There was a good deal of special skill required for the production of a flying-kite. It must be perfectly still and steady when at its highest flight in the air. Paper messengers were sent up to it along the string which held it to the ground. The top of the Calton Hill was the most favourite place for enjoying this pleasant amusement.

Another article for which I became equally famous was the manufacture of small brass cannon. These I cast and bored, and mounted on their appropriate gun-carriages. They proved very effective, especially in the loudness of the report when fired. I also converted large cellar-keys into a sort of hand-cannon. A touch-hole was bored into the barrel of the key, with a sliding brass collar that allowed the key-guns to be loaded and primed ready for firing.

The principal occasion on which the brass cannon and hand-guns were used was on the 4th of June—King George the

Third's birthday. This was always celebrated with exuberant and noisy loyalty.

My little brass cannon and hand-guns were very busy that day. They were fired until they became quite hot. These were the pre-lucifer days. The fire to light the powder at the touch-hole was obtained by the use of a flint, a steel, and a tinder-box. The flint was struck sharply on the steel; a drop of fire fell into the tinder-box, and the match of hemp string, soaked in salt-petre, was readily lit, and fired off the little guns.

I carried on quite a trade in forging beautiful little steels. I forged them out of old files, which proved excellent material for the purpose. I filed them up into neat and correct forms, and then hardened and tempered them at the little stove in my father's workroom, where of course there were also a suitable anvil, hammer, and tongs.

As I have said, I did not learn much at the High School. My mind was never opened up by what was taught me there. It was a mere matter of rote and cram. There was one thing, however, that I *did* learn at the High School. That was the blessing and advantage of friendship. There were several of my schoolfellows of a like disposition with myself, with whom I formed attachments which ended only with life. I may mention two of them in particular—Jemmy Patterson and Tom Smith. The former was the son of one of the largest iron-founders in Edinburgh. He was kind, good, and intelli-gent. He and I were great cronies. He took me to his father's workshops. Nothing could have been more agreeable to my tastes, for there I saw how iron castings were made. Mill-work and steam-engines were repaired there, and I could see the way in which power was produced and communi-cated. To me it was a most instructive school of practical mechanics. Although I was only about thirteen at the time, I used to lend a hand, in which hearty zeal made up for want of strength. I look back to these days, especially to the Saturday afternoons spent in the workshops of this admirably conducted iron foundry, as a most important part of my education as a mechanical engineer. I did not *read* about such things; for words were of little use. But I saw and handled, and thus all the ideas in connection with them became permanently rooted in my mind.

Each department of the iron foundry was superintended by an able and intelligent man. He was distinguished not only by his ability but by his steadiness and sobriety. The men were for the most part promoted to their foremanship from the ranks, and had been brought up in the concern from their boyhood. They possessed a strong individuality of character, and served their employer faithfully and loyally. One of these excellent men, with whom I was frequently brought into contact, was William Watson. He took special charge of all that related to the construction and repairs of steam-engines, water-wheels, and mill work generally. He was a skilful designer and draughtsman and an excellent pattern-maker. His designs were drawn in a bold and distinct style on large deal boards, and were passed into the hands of the mechanics to be translated by them into actual work.

It was no small privilege to me to stand by, and now and then hold the end of the long straight-edge, or by some humble but zealous genuine help of mine contribute to the progress of these substantial and most effective mechanical drawings. Watson explained to me, in the most common-sense manner, his reasons for the various forms, arrangements, and proportions of the details of his designs. He was an enthusiast on the subject of Euclid; and to see the beautiful problems applied by him in working out his excellent drawings was to me a lesson beyond all price.

Watson was effectively assisted by his two sons, who carried out their father's designs in the form of the wood patterns by which the foundry-men or moulders reproduced their shapes in cast iron, and the smiths by their craft realised the wrought-iron portions. These sons of Mr Watson were of that special class of workmen called mill-wrights—a class now almost extinct, though many of the best known engineers originally belonged to it. They could work with equal effectiveness in wood or iron.

One of the most original characters about the foundry, however, was Johnie Syme. He took charge of the old Boulton and Watt steam-engine which gave motion to the machinery of the works. It also produced the blast for the cupolas, in which the pig and cast iron scrap was daily melted, to be cast into the various objects produced in the foundry. Johnie was a complete incarnation of technical knowledge. He was the Jack-of-all-trades of the establishment, and the standing counsel in every out-of-the-way case of managing and overcoming mechanical difficulties. He was the superintendent of the boring machines. In those days the boring of a steam-engine cylinder was considered high art *in excelsis*! Patterson's firm was celebrated for the accuracy of its boring.

I owe Johnie Syme a special debt of gratitude, as it was he who first initiated me into that most important of all technical processes in practical mechanism—the art of hardening and tempering steel. It is, perhaps, not saying too much to assert that the successful practice of the mechanical arts, by means of which the civilised man rises above the savage condition, is due to that wonderful change. Man began with wood, and stone, and bone; he proceeded to bronze and iron; but it was only by means of hardened steel that he could accomplish anything in arms, in agriculture, or in architecture. The instant hardening which occurs on plunging a red-hot piece of steel into cold water may well be described as mysterious. Even in these

days,[1] when science has defined the causes of so many pheno-
mena, the reason of steel becoming hard on suddenly cooling it
down from a red heat, is a fact that no one has yet explained!
The steel may be *tempered* by modifying the degrees of heat to
which it is subsequently subjected. It may thus be toughened
by slightly reheating the hardened steel; the resoftening course
is indicated by certain prismatic tints, which appear in a peculiar
mode of succession on its surface. The skilful artisan knows by
experience the exact point at which it is necessary again to
plunge it into cold water in order to realise the requisite tough-
ness or hardness of the material required for his purposes.

In all these matters, my early instructor, Johnie Syme, gave
me such information as proved of the greatest use to me in the
after history of my mechanical career.

Tom Smith was another of my attached cronies. Our friendship began at the High School in 1818. A similarity of disposition bound us together. Smith was the son of an enterprising
general merchant at Leith. His father had a special genius for
practical chemistry, and had established an extensive colour
manufactury at Portobello, near Edinburgh, where he produced
white lead, red lead, and a great variety of colours—in the
preparation of which he acquired a thorough knowledge of
chemistry. Tom Smith inherited his father's tastes, and admitted me to share in his experiments, which were carried on
in a chemical laboratory situated behind his father's house at
the bottom of Leith Walk.

We had a special means of communication. When anything
particular was going on at the laboratory, Tom hoisted a white
flag on the top of a high pole in his father's garden. Though I
was more than a mile away, I kept a look-out in the direction
of the laboratory with a spy-glass. My father's house was at the
top of Leith Walk, and Smith's house was at the bottom of it.

[1] *About the year 1880.*

When the flag was hoisted I could clearly see the invitation to me to come down. I was only too glad to run down the Walk and join my chum, to take part in some interesting chemical process. Mr Smith, the father, made me heartily welcome. He was pleased to see his son so much attached to me, and he perhaps believed that I was worthy of his friendship. We took zealous part in all the chemical proceedings, and in that way Tom was fitting himself for the business of his life.

My friend Tom Smith and I made it a rule—and in this we were encouraged by his father—that, so far as was possible, we ourselves should actually *make* the acids and other substances used in our experiments. We were not to buy them ready made, as this would have taken the zest out of our enjoyment. We should have lost the pleasure and instruction of producing them by means of our own wits and energies. To encounter and overcome a difficulty is the most interesting of all things. Hence, though often baffled, we eventually produced perfect specimens of nitrous, nitric, and muriatic acids. We distilled alcohol from duly fermented sugar and water, and rectified the resultant spirit from fusel oil by passing the alcoholic vapour through animal charcoal before it entered the worm of the still. We converted part of the alcohol into sulphuric ether. We produced phosphorus from old bones and elaborated many of the mysteries of chemistry.

The amount of practical information which we obtained by this system of making our own chemical agents was such as to reward us, in many respects, for the labour we underwent. To outsiders it might appear a very troublesome and roundabout way of getting at the finally desired result. But I feel certain that there was no better method of rooting chemical or any other instruction deeply in our minds. Indeed, I regret that the same system is not pursued by the youth of the present day. They are seldom, if ever, called upon to exert their own wits and industry to obtain the requisites for their instruction.

I often observe, in shop-windows, every detail of model ships and model steam-engines supplied ready made for those who are 'said to be' of an ingenious and mechanical turn. Thus the vital uses of resourcefulness are done away with, and a sham exhibition of mechanical genius is paraded before you by the young impostors—the result, for the most part, of too free a supply of pocket money. I have known too many instances of parents being led by such false evidence of constructive skill to apprentice their sons to some engineering firm; and, after paying vast sums, finding out that the pretender comes out of the engineering shop with no other practical accomplishment than that of glove-wearing and cigar-smoking!

The truth is that the eyes and the fingers—*the bare fingers*—are the two principal inlets to sound practical instruction. They are the chief sources of trustworthy knowledge in all the materials and operations with which the engineer has to deal. No *book* knowledge can avail for that purpose. The nature and properties of the materials must come in through the finger ends.

CHAPTER III

Mechanical Beginnings: Model-making

I LEFT the High School at the end of 1820. I carried with me a small amount of Latin, and no Greek. I do not think I was much the better for my small acquaintance with the dead languages. I wanted something more living and quickening. I continued my studies at private classes. Arithmetic and geometry were my favourite branches. My father gave me every opportunity for practising the art of drawing. He taught me to sketch with exactness every object, whether natural or artificial, so as to enable the hand accurately to reproduce what the eye had seen. This accomplishment of accurate drawing, which I achieved for the most part in my father's workroom, served me many a good turn in future years with reference to the engineering work which became the business of my life.

I was constantly busy; mind, hands, and body were kept in a state of delightful and instructive activity. When not drawing, I occupied myself in my father's workshop at the lathe, the furnace, or the bench. I gradually became initiated into every variety of mechanical and chemical manipulation. I made my own tools and constructed my chemical apparatus, as far as lay in my power. With respect to the latter, I constructed a very handy and effective blowpipe apparatus, consisting of a small air force-pump, connected with a cylindrical vessel of tin plate. By means of an occasional use of the handy pump, it yielded such a fine steady blowpipe blast, as enabled me to melt glass tubes and blow bulbs for thermometers, to analyse metals or mineral substances, or to do any other work for which intense heat was necessary. My natural aptitude for manipulation, whether in mechanical or chemical operations, proved very serviceable to myself as well as to others; and (as will be shown hereafter) it gained for me the friendship of many distinguished scientific men.

In the autumn of 1823, when I was fifteen years old, I had a most delightful journey with my father. It was the first occasion on which I had been a considerable distance from home. And yet the journey was only to Stirling.

From Stirling we walked to Alloa, passing the picturesque cascades rushing down the clefts of the Ochils. But the most interesting thing that I saw during the journey was the Devon Ironworks. I had read and heard about the processes carried on there in smelting iron ore and running it into pig-iron. The origin of the familiar trade term 'pig-iron' is derived from the result of an arrangement most suitable for distributing the molten iron as it rushes forth from the opening made at the bottom part of the blast furnace, when, after its reduction from the ore, it collects in a fluid mass of several tons' weight. Previous to 'tapping' the furnace, a great central channel is made in the sand-covered floor of the forge; this central channel is then subdivided into many lateral branches or canals, into which the molten iron flows, and eventually hardens.

The great steam-engine that worked the blast furnace was the largest that I had ever seen. A singular expedient was employed at these works, of using a vast vault hewn in the solid rock of the hillside, for the purpose of storing up the blast produced by the engines, and so equalising the pressure; thus turning a mountain side into a reservoir for the use of a blast-furnace. This seemed to me a daring and wonderful engineering feat.

We waited at the works until the usual time had arrived for letting out the molten iron which had been accumulating at the lower part of the blast-furnace. It was a fine sight to see the stream of white-hot iron flowing like water into the large gutter immediately before the opening. From this the molten iron flowed on until it filled the moulds of sand which branched off from the central gutter. The iron left in the centre, when cooled and broken up, was called *sow* metal, while that in the branches was called *pig* iron; the terms being derived from the appearance of a sow engaged in its maternal duties. The pig-iron is thus cast in handy-sized pieces for the purpose of being transported to other iron-foundries; while the clumsy sow metal is broken up and passes through another process of melting, or is reserved for foundry uses at the works where it is produced. After inspecting with great pleasure the machinery connected with the foundry, we took our leave and returned to Edinburgh by steamer from Alloa.

Shortly after, I had the good fortune to make the acquaintance of Robert Bald, the well-known mining engineer. He was one of the most kind-hearted men I have ever known. He was always ready to communicate his knowledge to young and old.

On several occasions he wished me to accompany him on his business journeys, in order that I might see some works that would supply me with valuable information. He had designed a powerful pumping engine to drain more effectually a large colliery district near Bannockburn—close to the site of the great battle in the time of Robert the Bruce. He invited me to join him. It was with the greatest pleasure that I accepted his invitation; for there would be not only the pleasure of seeing a noble piece of steam machinery brought into action for the first time, but also the enjoyment of visiting the celebrated Carron Ironworks.

The Carron Ironworks are classic ground to engineers. They are associated with the memory of Roebuck, Watt, and Miller of Dalswinton. For there Roebuck and Watt began the first working steam-engine; Miller applied the steam-engine to the purposes of navigation, and invented the Carronade gun. The works existed at an early period in the history of British iron manufacture. Much of the machinery continued to be of wood. Although effective in a general way it was monstrously cumbrous. It gave the idea of vast power and capability of resistance, while it was far from being so in reality. It was, however, truly imposing and impressive in its effect upon strangers. When seen partially lit up by the glowing masses of white-hot iron, with only the rays of bright sunshine gleaming through the holes in the roof, and the dark, smoky vaults in which the cumbrous machinery was heard rumbling away in the distance —while the moving parts were dimly seen through the murky atmosphere, mixed with the sounds of escaping steam and rushes of water; with the half-naked men darting about with masses of red-hot iron and ladles full of molten iron—it made a powerful impression upon the mind.

To return to my life at Edinburgh: I was now seventeen years old. I had acquired a considerable amount of practical knowledge as to the use and handling of mechanical tools, and I desired to turn it to some account. I was able to construct working models of steam-engines and other apparatus required for the illustration of mechanical subjects. I began by making a small working steam-engine for the purpose of grinding the oil-colours used by my father in his artistic work. The result was quite satisfactory. Many persons came to see my active little steam-engine at work, and they were so pleased with it that I received several orders for small workshop engines, and also for some models of steam-engines to illustrate the subjects taught at Mechanics' Institutions.

I contrived a sectional model of a complete condensing steam-engine of the beam and parallel motion construction. The model, as seen from one side, exhibited every external detail in full and due action when the flywheel was moved round by hand; while, on the other or sectional side, every detail of the interior was seen, with the steam-valves and air-pump as well as the motion of the piston in the cylinder, with the construction of the piston and the stuffing box, together with the slide-valve and steam passages, all in due position and relative movement.

The first of these sectional models of the steam-engine was made for the Edinburgh School of Arts, where its uses in instructing mechanics and others in the application of steam were highly appreciated. The second was made for Professor Leslie, of the Edinburgh University, for use in his lectures on Natural Philosophy. He was so pleased with my addition to his class-room apparatus, that, besides expressing his great thanks for my services, he most handsomely presented me with a free ticket to his Natural Philosophy class as a regular student, so long as it suited me to make use of his instruction.   I had every reason to consider his friendship and his teaching as amongst the most important elements in my future success as a practical engineer.

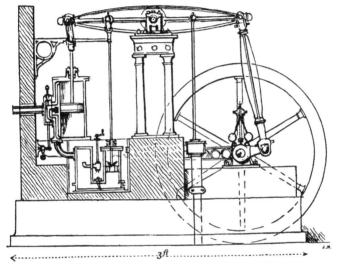

A Drawing by James Nasmyth of one of his
Steam-Engine Models

The successful establishment of the Edinburgh School of Arts had a considerable effect throughout the country.   Similar institutions were established.   Lectures were delivered, and the necessary illustrations were acquired—above all, working models of the steam-engine.   There was quite a run upon me for supplying them.   The price I charged for my models was £10; and with the pecuniary results I made over one-third to my father, as a sort of help to remunerate him for my 'keep', and with the rest I purchased tickets of admission to certain classes in the University. What with my attendance upon the classes, and my workshop and drawing occupations, my time did not hang heavily on my hands.

I got up early in the mornings to work at my father's lathe, and I sat up late at night to do the brass castings in my bed-room. Some of this, however, I did during the day-time, when not attending the University classes. The way in which I con-verted my bedroom into a brass foundry was as follows: I took up the carpet so that there might be nothing but the bare boards to be injured by the heat. My furnace in the grate was made of four plates of stout sheet iron, lined with fire-brick, corner to corner. To get the requisite sharp draught I bricked up with single bricks the front of the fireplace, leaving a hole at the back of the furnace for the short pipe just to fit into. The fuel was generally gas coke and cinders saved from the kitchen. The heat I raised was superb—a white heat, sufficient to melt in a crucible six or eight pounds of brass.

Then I had a box of moulding sand, where the moulds were gently rammed in around the pattern previous to the casting. But how did I get my brass? All the old brass-work in my father's workshop drawers and boxes was laid under contribu-tion. This brass being for the most part soft and yellow, I made it extra hard by the addition of a due proportion of tin. It was then capable of taking a pure finished edge. When I had ex-hausted the stock of old brass, I had to buy old copper or new in the form of ingot or tile copper, and when melted I added to it one-seventh of its weight of pure tin, which yielded the strongest alloy of the two metals. When cast into any required form this was a treat to work, so sound and close was the grain, and so durable in resisting wear and tear. This is the true bronze or gun-metal.

When melted, the liquid brass was let into the openings, until the whole of the moulds were filled. After the metal cooled it was taken out; and when the room was sorted up no one could have known that my foundry operations had been carried on in my bedroom. My brass foundry was right over my father's bedroom. He had forbidden me to work late at night, as I did occasionally on the sly. Sometimes when I ought to have been asleep I was detected by the sound of the ramming-in of the sand of the moulding boxes. On such occasions my father let me know that I was disobeying his orders by rapping on the ceiling of his bedroom with a slight wooden rod of ten feet that he kept for measuring purposes. But I got over that difficulty by placing a bit of old carpet under my moulding boxes as a non-conductor of sound, so that no ramming could afterwards be heard. My dear mother also was afraid that I should damage my health by working so continuously. She would come into the workroom late in the evening, when I was working at the lathe or the vice, and say, 'Ye'll kill yourself, laddie, by working so hard and so late'. Yet she took a great pride in seeing me so busy and so happy.

Nearly the whole of my steam-engine models were made in my father's workroom. His foot-lathe and stove, together with my brass casting arrangements in my bedroom, answered all my purposes in the way of model-making. But I had at times to avail myself of the smithy and foundry that my kind and worthy friend, George Douglass, had established in the neighbourhood. He had begun business as a 'jobbing smith', but being a most intelligent and energetic workman, he shot ahead and laid the foundations of a large trade in steam-engines. When I had any part of a job in hand that was beyond the capabilities of my father's lathe, or my bedroom casting apparatus, I immediately went to Douglass's smithy, where every opportunity was afforded me for carrying on my larger class of work.

His place was only about five minutes' walk from my father's house. I had the use of his large turning-lathe, which was much more suitable for big or heavy work than the lathe at home. When any considerable bit of steel or iron forging had to be done, a forge fire and anvil were always placed at my service. In making my flywheels for the sectional models of steam-engines I had a rather neat and handy way of constructing them. The boss of the wheel of brass was nicely bored; the arm-holes were carefully drilled and tapped, so as to allow the arms which I had turned to be screwed in and appear like neat columns of round wrought-iron or steel screwed into the boss of the flywheel.

In return for the great kindness of George Douglass in allowing me to have the use of his foundry, I resolved to present him with a specimen of my handiwork. I desired to try my powers in making a more powerful steam-engine than I had as yet attempted to construct, in order to drive the large turning-lathe and the other tools and machinery of his small foundry. I accordingly set to work and constructed a direct-acting high-pressure steam-engine, with a cylinder four inches in diameter. I use the term direct-acting, because I dispensed with the beam and parallel motion, which was generally considered the correct mode of transferring the action of the piston to the crank.

The result of my labours was a very efficient steam-engine, which set all the lathes and mechanical tools in brisk activity of movement. It had such an enlivening effect upon the workmen that George Douglass afterwards told me that the busy hum of the wheels, and the active, smooth, rhythmic sound of the merry little engine had, through some sympathetic agency, so quickened the strokes of every hammer, chisel, and file in his workmen's hands, that it nearly doubled the output of work for the same wages!

About the year 1827, when I was nineteen years old, the

subject of steam-carriages to run upon common roads occupied considerable attention. Several engineers and mechanical schemers had tried their hands, but as yet no substantial results had come of their attempts to solve the problem. Like others, I tried my hand. Having made a small working model of a

Nasmyth's Road Steam-carriage

steam-carriage, I exhibited it before the members of the Scottish Society of Arts. The performance of this active little machine was so gratifying to the Society that they requested me to construct one of such power as to enable four or six persons to be conveyed along the ordinary roads. The members of the Society, in their individual capacity, subscribed £60, which they placed in my hands as the means of carrying out their project.

I accordingly set to work at once. I had the heavy parts of

the engine and carriage done at Anderson's foundry at Leith. Anderson possessed some excellent tools, which enabled me to proceed rapidly with the work. Besides, he was most friendly, and took much delight in being concerned in my enterprise. This 'big job' was executed in about four months. The steam-carriage was completed and exhibited before the members of the Society of Arts. Many successful trials were made with it on the Queensferry Road, near Edinburgh. The runs were generally of four or five miles, with a load of eight passengers sitting on benches about three feet from the ground.

The experiments were continued for nearly three months, to the great satisfaction of the members. I may mention that in my steam-carriage I employed the waste steam to create a blast or draught by discharging it into the short chimney of the boiler at its lowest part, and found it most effective. I was not at that time aware that George Stephenson and others had adopted the same method; but it was afterwards gratifying to me to find that I had been correct as regards the important uses of the steam blast in the chimney.

The Society of Arts did not attach any commercial value to my steam road-carriage. It was merely as a matter of experiment that they had invited me to construct it. When it proved successful they made me a present of the entire apparatus. As I was anxious to get on with my studies, and to prepare for the work of practical engineering, I proceeded no further. I broke up the steam-carriage and sold the two small high-pressure engines, provided with a compact and strong boiler, for £67, a sum which more than defrayed all the expenses of the construction and working of the machine.

I still continued to make investigations as to the powers and capabilities of the steam-engine. There were numerous breweries, distilleries, and other establishments near Edinburgh where such engines were at work. As they were made by different engineers, I was desirous of seeing them and making sketches of them, especially when there was any special peculiarity in their construction. I found this a most favourite and instructive occupation. The engine-tenders became very friendly with me, and they were always glad to see me interested in them and their engines. They were especially delighted to see me make 'drafts', as they called my sketches, of the engines under their charge.

CHAPTER IV

I become Maudsley's Assistant

I N the course of my inspection of the engines made by different makers I was impressed with the superiority of those made by the Carmichaels of Dundee. They were excellent both in design and in execution. I afterwards found that the Carmichaels were among the first of the Scottish engine-makers who gave due attention to the employment of improved mechanical tools, with the object of producing accurate work with greater ease, rapidity and economy, than could possibly be effected by the hand labour of even the most skilful workmen. I was told that the cause of the excellence of the Carmichaels' work was not only in the ability of the heads of the firm, but in their employment of the best engineers' tools. Some of their leading men had worked at Maudsley's machine shop in London, the fame of which had already reached Dundee; and Maudsley's system of employing machine tools had been imported into the northern steam factory.

I had on many occasions, when visiting the works where steam-engines were employed, heard of the name and fame of Maudsley. I was told that his works were the very centre and climax of all that was excellent in mechanical workmanship. These reports built up in my mind, at this early period of my aspirations, an earnest and hopeful desire that I might some day get a sight of Maudsley's celebrated works in London. In course of time it developed into a passion. I will proceed to show how my inmost desires were satisfied.

The chief object of my ambition was now to be taken on at Henry Maudsley's works in London. I had heard so much of his engineering work, of his assortment of machine-making tools, and of the admirable organisation of his manufactory, that I longed to obtain employment there. I was willing to labour, in however humble a capacity, in that far-famed workshop.

I was aware that my father had not the means of paying the large premium required for placing me as an apprentice at Maudsley's works. I was also informed that Maudsley had ceased to take pupils. After experience, he had found that the premium apprentices caused him much annoyance and irritation. They came in 'gloves'; their attendance was irregular; they spread a bad example amongst the regular apprentices and workmen; and on the whole they were found to be very disturbing elements in the work of the factory.

It therefore occurred to me that, by showing some specimens of my work and drawings, I might be able to satisfy Mr Maudsley that I was not an amateur, but a regular working engineer. With this object I set to work, and made with special care a most complete working model of a high-pressure engine. The cylinder was 2 inches diameter, and the stroke 6 inches. Every part of the engine, including the patterns, the castings, the forgings, was the result of my own individual handiwork. I turned out this sample of my ability as an engineer workman in such a style as even now I should be proud to own.

In like manner I executed several specimens of my ability as a mechanical draughtsman; for I knew that Maudsley would thoroughly understand my ability to work from a plan. Mechanical drawing is the alphabet of the engineer. Without this the workman is merely a 'hand'. With it he indicates the possession of a 'head'. I also made some samples of my skill in hand-sketching of machines and parts of machines in perspective—that is, as such objects really appear when set before us in their normal aspect. I was the more desirous of exhibiting the ability which I possessed in mechanical draughtsmanship, as I knew it to be a somewhat rare and much-valued acquirement.

Having thus provided myself with such visible and tangible evidences of my capabilities as a young engineer, I carefully packed up my working model and drawings, and prepared to start for London. On the 19th of May 1829, accompanied by my father, I set sail by the Leith smack *Edinburgh Castle*, Captain Orr, master. After a pleasant voyage of four days we reached the mouth of the Thames. We sailed up from the Nore on Saturday afternoon, lifted up, as it were, by the tide, for it was almost a dead calm the whole way.

The tide, which had carried us up the river as far as Woolwich, suddenly turned; and we remained there during the night. Early next morning the tide rose, and we sailed away again. It was a bright mild morning. The sun came 'dancing up the east' as we floated past wharfs and woodyards and old houses on the banks, past wherries and coal-boats and merchant-ships on the river, until we reached our destination at the Irongate Wharf, nearly opposite the Tower of London. I heard St Paul's clock strike six just as we reached our mooring ground.

Captain Orr was kind enough to allow us to make the ship our hotel during the Sunday, as it was by no means convenient for us to remove our luggage on that day.

On the following day my father and I set out in search of lodgings, hotels being at that time beyond our economical method of living. We succeeded in securing a tidy lodging at No. 14 Agnes Place, Waterloo Road. The locality had a special attraction for me, as it was not far from that focus of interest— Maudsley's factory. Our luggage was removed from the ship to the lodgings, and my ponderous cases, containing the examples of my skill as an engineer workman, were deposited in a carpenter's workshop close at hand.

I was now anxious for the interview with Maudsley. My father had been introduced to him by a mutual friend some two or three years before, and that was enough. On the morning of May the 26th we set out together, and reached his house in Westminster Road, Lambeth. It adjoined his factory. My father knocked at the door. My own heart beat fast. Would he be at home? Would he receive us? Yes! he was at home; and we were invited to enter.

Mr Maudsley received us in the most kind and frank manner. After a little conversation my father explained the object of his visit. 'My son', he said, pointing to me, 'is very anxious to have the opportunity of acquiring a thorough practical knowledge of mechanical engineering, by serving as an apprentice in some such establishment as yours.' 'Well,' replied Maudsley, 'I must frankly confess to you that my experience of pupil apprentices has been so unsatisfactory that my partner and myself have determined to discontinue to receive them—no matter at what premium.' This was a very painful blow to myself; for it seemed to put an end to my sanguine expectations.

Mr Maudsley knew that my father was interested in all matters relating to mechanical engineering, and he courteously invited him to go round the works. Of course I accompanied them. The sight of the workshops astonished me. They excelled all that I had anticipated. The beautiful machine tools, the silent smooth whirl of the machinery, the active movements of the men, the excellent quality of the work in progress, and the admirable order and management that pervaded the whole establishment, rendered me more tremblingly anxious than ever to obtain some employment *there*, in however humble a capacity.

Mr Maudsley observed the earnest interest which I and my father took in everything going on, and explained the movements of the machinery and the rationale of the proceedings in the most lively and kindly manner. It was while we were passing from one part of the factory to another that I observed the beautiful steam-engine which gave motion to the tools and machinery of the workshops. The man who attended it was engaged in cleaning out the ashes from under the boiler furnace, in order to wheel them away to their place outside. On the spur of the moment I said to Mr Maudsley, 'If you would only permit me to do such a job as that in your service, I should consider myself most fortunate!' I shall never forget the keen but kindly look that he gave me. 'So', said he, 'you are one of that sort, are you?' I was inwardly delighted at his words.

When our round of the works was concluded, I ventured to say to Mr Maudsley that I had brought up with me from Edinburgh some working models of steam-engines and mechanical drawings, and I should feel truly obliged if he would allow me to show them to him. 'By all means,' said he; 'bring them to me to-morrow at twelve o'clock.' I need not say how much pleased I was at this permission to exhibit my handiwork, and how anxious I felt as to the result of Mr Maudsley's inspection of it.

I carefully unpacked my working model of the steam-engine at the carpenter's shop, and had it conveyed, together with my drawings, on a hand-cart to Mr Maudsley's next morning at the appointed hour. I was allowed to place my work for his inspection in a room next his office and counting-house. I then called at his residence close by, where he kindly received me in his library. He asked me to wait until he and his partner, Joshua Field, had inspected my handiwork.

I waited anxiously. Twenty long minutes passed. At last he entered the room, and from a lively expression in his countenance I observed in a moment that the great object of my long-cherished ambition had been obtained! He expressed, in good round terms, his satisfaction at my practical ability as a workman engineer and mechanical draughtsman. Then, opening the door which led from his library into his beautiful private workshop, he said, 'This is where I wish you to work, beside me, as my assistant workman. From what I have seen there is no need of an apprenticeship in your case'.

He then proceeded to show me the collection of exquisite tools of all sorts with which his private workshop was stored. They mostly bore the impress of his own clearheadedness and common-sense. The workshop was surrounded with cabinets and drawers, filled with evidences of the master's skill and industry. Every tool had a purpose. It had been invented for some special reason. Sometimes it struck the keynote, as it were, to many of the important contrivances which enable man to obtain a complete mastery over materials.

There were also hung upon the walls, or placed upon shelves, many treasured relics of the first embodiments of his constructive genius. There were many models explaining, step by step, the gradual progress of his teeming inventions and contrivances. The workshop was thus quite a historical museum of mechanism. It exhibited his characteristic qualities in construction. I afterwards found out that many of the contrivances preserved in his private workshop were treasured as suggestive of some interesting early passage in his useful and active life. They were kept as relics of his progress towards mechanical perfection.

It was one of his favourite maxims, 'First, *get a clear notion* of what you desire to accomplish, and then in all probability you

PLATE I

ONE OF MAUDSLEY'S TREADLE LATHES

GENERAL VIEW

(By permission, Science Museum, South Kensington)

will succeed in doing it'. Another was 'Keep a sharp look-out upon your materials; get rid of every pound of material you can *do without*; put to yourself the question, "What business has it to be there?"; avoid complexities, and make everything as simple as possible'.

Mr Maudsley seemed at once to take me into his confidence. He treated me in the most kindly manner—not as a workman or an apprentice but as a friend. I was an anxious listener to everything that he said; and it gave him pleasure to observe that I understood and valued his conversation. The greatest treat of all was in store for me. He showed me his exquisite collection of taps and dies and screw-tackle, which he had made with the utmost care for his own service. It rested in a succession of drawers near to the bench where he worked. There was a place for every article, and every one was in its place. There was a look of tidiness about the collection which was very characteristic of the man. Order was one of the rules which he rigidly observed, and he endeavoured to enforce it upon all who were in his employment.

He proceeded to dilate upon the importance of the uniformity of screws. Some may call it an improvement, but it might almost be called a revolution in mechanical engineering which Mr Maudsley introduced. Before his time no system had been followed in proportioning the number of threads of a screw to its diameter. Every bolt and nut was thus a speciality in itself, and neither possessed nor admitted of any community with its neighbours. To such an extent had this practice been carried that all bolts and their corresponding nuts had to be specially marked as belonging to each other. Any intermixture that occurred between them led to endless trouble and expense, as well as inefficiency and confusion—especially when parts of complex machines had to be taken to pieces for repairs.

None but those who lived in the comparatively early days of

machine manufacture can form an adequate idea of the annoyance, delay, and cost of this utter want of system, or can appreciate the vast services rendered to mechanical engineering by Mr Maudsley, who was the first to introduce the practical measures necessary for its remedy. In his system of screw-cutting machinery, and in his taps and dies and screw-tackle generally, he set the example, and in fact laid the foundation, of all that has since been done in this most essential branch of machine construction.

Mr Maudsley kept me with him for about three hours, initiating me into his system. It was with the greatest delight that I listened to his wise instruction. The sight of his excellent tools, which he showed me one by one, filled me with an almost painful feeling of earnest hope that I might be able in any degree practically to express how thankful I was to be admitted to so invaluable a privilege as to be in close communication with this great master in all that was most perfect in practical mechanics.

When he concluded his exposition, he told me in the most kindly manner that it would be well for me to take advantage of my father's presence in London to obtain some general knowledge of the metropolis, to see the most remarkable buildings, and to obtain an introduction to some of my father's friends. He gave me a week for this purpose, and said he should be glad to see me at his workshop on the following Monday week.

It singularly happened that on the first day my father went out with me he encountered an old friend. This was no other than Henry Brougham.[1] He was descending the steps leading into St James' Park, from the place where the Duke of York's monument now stands. Brougham immediately recognised my

[1] *Henry Brougham, afterwards Lord Brougham, a native of Edinburgh, was a famous lawyer, politician and writer, who was interested in science by way of recreation. He was Lord Chancellor of England from 1830 to 1834.*

father. There was a hearty shaking of hands, and many inquiries on either side. 'And what brings you to London now?' asked Brougham. My father told him that it was about his son here, who had obtained an important position at Maudsley's the engineer's.

'If I can do anything for you,' said Brougham, addressing me, 'let me know. It will afford me much pleasure to give you introductions to men of science in London.' I ventured to say that of all the men of science in London I most wished to see Mr Faraday of the Royal Institution. 'Well,' said Brougham, 'I will send you a letter of introduction.' We then parted.

On returning home to our lodgings that evening we found a note from Brougham, enclosing letters of introduction to Faraday and other scientific men, and stating that if at any time he could be of service to me he hoped that I would at once make use of him. My father was truly gratified with the substantial evidence of Brougham's kindly remembrance of him; and I? how could I be grateful enough? not only for my father's never-failing attention to my growth in knowledge and wisdom, but to his ever-willing readiness to help me onward in the path of scientific working and mechanical engineering.

CHAPTER V

Maudsley's Works

ON the morning of Monday, the 30th of May 1829, I commenced my regular attendance at Mr Maudsley's workshop. My first job was to assist him in making some modifications in the details of a machine which he had contrived some years before for generating original screws. I use the word 'generating' as being most appropriate to express the objects and results of one of Mr Maudsley's most original inventions.

It consisted in the employment of a knife-edged hardened steel instrument, so arranged as to be set at any required angle, and its edge caused to penetrate the surface of a cylindrical bar of soft steel or brass. This bar being revolved under the incisive action of the angularly placed knife-edged instrument, it thus received a continuous spiral groove cut into its surface. It was then in the condition of a rudimentary screw.

The spiral groove, thus generated, was deepened to the required extent by a suitable and pointed hard steel tool firmly held in the jaws of an adjustable slide made for the purpose, as part and parcel of the bed of the machine. In the case of square-threaded screws being required, a square-pointed tool was employed in place of the V or angle-threaded tool. And in order to generate or produce right-hand or left-hand screws, all that was necessary was to set the knife-edged instrument to a right or left hand inclination in respect to the axis of the cylindrical bar at the outset of the operation.

This beautiful and truly original contrivance became, in the hands of its inventor, the parent of a vast progeny of perfect screws, whose descendants are to be found in every workshop throughout the world, wherever first-class machinery is constructed. The production of perfect screws was one of Maudsley's highest ambitions and his principal technical achievement. It was a type of his invaluable faculty of solving the most difficult problems by the most direct and simple methods.

It was by the same method that he produced the Guide screw. His screw-cutting lathe was moved by combination wheels, and by its means he could, by the one Guide screw, obtain screws of every variety of pitch and diameter. As an illustration of its complete accuracy I may mention that by its means a screw of five feet in length and two inches in diameter was cut with fifty

PLATE II

HEADSTOCK AND SLIDE-REST OF ONE OF
MAUDSLEY'S TREADLE LATHES

MAUDSLEY'S SCREW-GENERATING MACHINE
(*Both by permission, Science Museum, South Kensington*)

threads to the inch; the nut to fit on to it being twelve inches long, and containing six hundred threads! This screw was principally used for dividing scales for astronomical and other metrical purposes of the highest class. By its means divisions were produced with such minuteness that they could only be seen by a microscope.

This screw was sent for exhibition to the Society of Arts. It is still[1] preserved with the utmost care at the Lambeth Works amongst the many admirable specimens of Henry Maudsley's inventive genius and delicate handiwork. Every skilled mechanic must thoroughly enjoy the sight of it, especially when he knows that it was not produced by an exceptional tool, but by the machine that was daily employed in the ordinary work of the factory.

I must not, however, omit to say that I took an early opportunity of presenting Brougham's letter of introduction to Faraday at the Royal Institution. I was received most cordially by that noble-minded man, whose face beamed with goodness and kindness. After some pleasant conversation he said he would call upon me at Maudsley's, whom he knew very well. Not long after Faraday called, and found me working beside Maudsley in his beautiful little workshop. A vice had been fitted up for me at the bench where he himself daily worked. Faraday expressed himself as delighted to find me in so enviable a position. He congratulated me on my special good fortune in having the inestimable advantage of being associated as assistant workman with one of the greatest mechanical engineers of the day.

Mr Maudsley offered to conduct Faraday through his workshops, and I was permitted to accompany them. I was much impressed with the intelligent conversation of Faraday, not only with the quickness he exhibited in appreciating the general

[1] *In the year 1878.*

excellence of the design and execution of the works in progress, but with his capacity for entering into the technical details of the composite tools and machinery which he saw during his progress through the place. This most pleasant and memorable meeting with the great philosopher initiated a friendship which I had the good fortune to continue until the close of his life.

It was, of course, an immense advantage for me to be so intimately associated with Mr Maudsley in carrying on his experimental work. I was not, however, his apprentice, but his assistant workman. It was necessary, therefore, in his opinion, that I should receive some remuneration for my services. Accordingly, at the conclusion of my first week in his service, he desired me to go to his chief cashier and arrange with him for receiving whatever amount of weekly wages I might consider satisfactory. I went to the counting-house and had an interview with Mr Young the cashier, a most worthy man. Knowing as I did the great advantages of my situation, and having a very modest notion of my own worthiness to occupy it, I said, in answer to Mr Young's question as to the amount of wages I desired, that if he did not think ten shillings a week too much I could do well enough with that. 'Very well,' said he, 'let it be so'. And he handed me half a sovereign!

I had determined, after I obtained a situation, not to cost my father another shilling. I knew how many calls he had upon him, at a time when he had his own numerous household to maintain. I therefore resolved, now that I had begun life on my own resources, to maintain myself, and to help him rather than be helped any longer. Thus the first half-sovereign I received from Mr Young was a great event in my life. It was the first wage as such, that I had ever received. I well remember the high satisfaction I felt as I carried it home to my lodgings; and all the more so as I was quite certain that I could, by strict economy and good management, contrive to make this weekly sum of ten shillings meet all my current expenses.

To return to my employment under Mr Maudsley. One of the early jobs that I undertook was in assisting him to make a beautiful small model of a pair of 200 horse-power marine steam-engines. The engines were then in course of construction in the factory. They were considered a bold advance on the marine engines then in use, not only in regard to their great power, but in containing many specialities in their details and general structure. Mr Maudsley had embodied so much of his thought in the design that he desired to have an exact model of them placed in his library, so as to keep a visible record of his ideas constantly before him. In fact, these engines might be regarded as the culmination of his constructive abilities.

In preparing the model it was necessary that everything should be made in exact conformity with the original. There were about three hundred minute bolts and nuts to be reduced to the proportional size. I esteemed it a great compliment to be entrusted with their execution. They were all to be made of cast-steel, and the nuts had to be cut to exact hexagonal form. Many of them had collars. To produce them by the use of the file in the ordinary mode would not only have been difficult and tedious, but in some cases practically impossible.

To get rid of the difficulty I suggested to Mr Maudsley a contrivance of my own by means of which the most rigid exactness in size as well as form could be given to these hexagonal nuts. He readily granted his permission. I constructed a special apparatus, consisting of a hard steel circular cutter to act as a circular file. When brought into operation in the production of these minute six-sided collared nuts, held firm in the spindle of a small dividing plate and attached to the slide-rest, each side was brought in succession under the action of the circular file or cutter with the most exact precision in regard to the division of the six sides. The result was absolutely perfect as respects the exactness of the six equal sides of the hexagonal nut, as well as their precise position in regard to the collar that was of one solid piece with it.

There was no great amount of ingenuity required in contriving this special tool, or in adapting it to the slide-rest of the lathe, to whose spindle end the file or cutter was fixed. But the result was so satisfactory, as regards both the accuracy and rapidity of execution in comparison with the usual process of hand filing, that Mr Maudsley was greatly pleased with the arrangement as well as with my zeal in contriving and executing this clever little tool. An enlarged edition of this collar-nut cutting machine was soon after introduced into the factory. It was one of the specialities that I adopted in my own workshop when I commenced business for myself, and it was eagerly adopted by mechanical engineers, whom we abundantly supplied with this special machine.

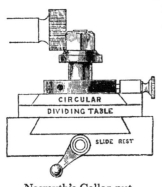

Nasmyth's Collar-nut Cutting Machine
(a) *Arrangement of Cutter and Slide-rest*

It was an inestimable advantage to me to be so intimately associated with this great mechanic. He was so invariably kind, pleasant and congenial. He communicated an infinite number of what he humorously called 'wrinkles', which afterwards proved of great use to me. My working hours usually terminated at six in the evening. But as many of the departments of the factory were often in full operation during busy times until eight o'clock, I went through them to observe the work while in progress. On these occasions I often met 'the

guv'nor' as the workmen called Mr Maudsley. He was going
his round of inspection, and when there was any special work
in hand he would call me up to him and explain any point in
connection with it that was worthy of particular notice. I
found this valuable privilege most instructive, as I obtained
from the chief mechanic himself a full insight into the methods,
means, and processes by which the skilful workmen advanced

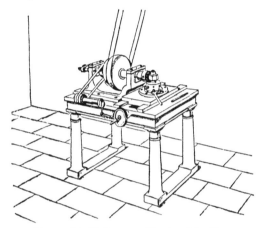

Nasmyth's Collar-nut Cutting Machine
(b) *General view of the Machine*

the various classes of work. I was also permitted to take notes
and make rapid sketches of any object that specially interested
me. The entire establishment thus became to me a school of
practical engineering of the most instructive kind.

To be permitted to stand by and observe the systematic way
in which Mr Maudsley would first mark or line out his work,
and the masterly manner in which he would deal with his
materials and cause them to assume the desired forms, was a
treat beyond all expression. Every stroke of the hammer,

chisel, or file told as an effective step towards the intended result. It was a never-to-be-forgotten practical lesson in workmanship, in the most exalted sense of the term.

The innate love of truth and accuracy which distinguished Mr Maudsley led him to value highly that class of technical dexterity in engineering workmen which enabled them to produce those details of mechanical structures in which perfectly flat or true plane surfaces were required. This was an essential condition for the effective and durable performance of their functions. Sometimes this was effected by the aid of the turning-lathe and slide-rest. But in most cases the object was attained by the dexterous use of the file, so that 'flat filing' then was, as it still is, one of the highest qualities of the skilled workman. No one that I ever met with could go beyond Henry Maudsley himself in his dexterous use of the file. By a few masterly strokes he could produce plane surfaces so true that when their accuracy was tested by a standard plane surface of absolute truth, they were never found defective; neither convex, nor concave, nor 'cross-winding'—that is, twisted.

The importance of having such standard planes caused him to have many of them placed on the benches beside his workmen, by means of which they might at once conveniently test their work. Three of each were made at a time, so that by the mutual rubbing of each on each the projecting surfaces were effaced. When the surfaces approached very near to the true plane, the still projecting minute points were carefully reduced by hard steel scrapers, until at last the standard plane surface was secured. When placed over each other they would float upon the thin stratum of air between them until dislodged by time and pressure. When they adhered closely to each other, they could only be separated by sliding each off each. This art of producing absolutely plane surfaces is, I believe, a very old mechanical 'dodge'. But, as employed by Maudsley's men, it greatly contributed to the improvement of the work turned out. It was used for the surfaces of slide valves, or wherever absolutely true plane surfaces were essential to the attainment of the best results, not only in the machinery turned out, but in educating the taste of his men towards first-class workmanship.

Maudsley's love of accuracy also led him to distrust the verdicts given by the employment of the ordinary callipers and compasses in determining the absolute or relative dimensions of the refined mechanism which he delighted to construct with his own hands. So much depended upon the manner in which the ordinary measuring instruments were handled and applied

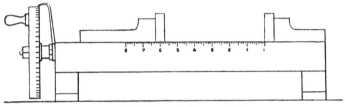

Maudsley's 'Lord Chancellor'

that they sometimes failed to give the required verdict as to accuracy. In order, therefore, to get rid of all difficulties in this respect, he designed and constructed a very compact and handy instrument which he always had on his bench beside his vice. He could thus, in a most accurate and rapid manner, obtain the most reliable evidence as to the relative dimensions, in length, width, or diameter, of any work which he had in hand. In consequence of the absolute truth of the verdicts of the instrument, he considered it as a Court of Final Appeal, and humorously called it 'The Lord Chancellor'.

This trustworthy 'Companion of the Bench' consisted of a very substantial and inflexible bed or base of hard brass. At one end of it was a perfectly hardened steel surface plate, having an absolutely true flat or plane face, against which one end or side of the object to be measured was placed; whilst a similar absolutely true plane surface of hardened steel was advanced by means of a suitable fine thread screw, until the object to be measured was just delicately in contact with it. The object was, as it were, between the jaws of a vice, but without any squeeze— being just free, which could be easily ascertained by feeling. These two absolutely plane surfaces, between which the object lay, had their distances apart easily read off from the scale engraved on the bed of the instrument, in inches and tenth parts of an inch, while the disk-head or handle of the screw was divided on its edge rim into hundredth or thousandth parts, as these bore an exact metrical relation to the pitch of the screw that moved the parallel steel faces of the measuring vice (as I may term it) nearer or farther apart.[1]

Not only absolute measure could be obtained by this means, but also the amount of minute differences could be ascertained with a degree of exactness that went quite beyond all the requirements of engineering mechanism; such, for instance, as the thousandth part of an inch! It might also have been divided so far as a millionth part of an inch, but these infinitesimal fractions have really nothing to do with the effective machinery that comes forth from our workshops, and merely show the mastery we possess over materials and mechanical forms.

[1] *This apparatus was really a large form of the Screw Micrometer which is widely used in modern engineering.*

CHAPTER VI

My Journey to the North: Death of Maudsley

IN the autumn of 1830 Mr Maudsley went to Berlin for the purpose of superintending the erection of machinery at the Royal Mint there. He intended to be absent from London for about a month; and he kindly permitted me to take my holiday during that period.

I had been greatly interested by the descriptions in the newspapers of the locomotive competition at Rainhill, near Liverpool. I was, therefore, exceedingly anxious to see Stephenson's 'Rocket', the engine that had won the prize. Taking with me letters of introduction from Mr Maudsley to persons of influence at Liverpool, I left London for the north on the afternoon of Saturday the 9th of September 1830. I took my place on the outside of the Liverpool coach, which set out from 'The Swan with Two Necks', in Lad Lane, City, one of the most celebrated coach-offices in those days.

The coach reached Liverpool on Sunday night. Next morning, without loss of time, I made my way to the then terminus of the Liverpool and Manchester Railway; and there, for the first time, I saw the famous 'Rocket'. The interest with which I beheld this distinguished and celebrated engine was much enhanced by seeing it make several short trial trips under the personal management of George Stephenson, who acted as engineman, while his son Robert acted as stoker. During their trips of four or five miles along the line the 'Rocket' attained the speed of thirty miles an hour—a speed then thought almost incredible! It was to me a most memorable and interesting sight, especially to see the father and son so appropriately engaged in working the engine that was to effect so great a change in the communications of the civilised world.

With the desire of seeing as much as possible of all that was interesting in the mechanical, architectural, and picturesque line on my return journey to London, I determined to walk, halting here and there by the way. The season of the year and the state of the weather were favourable for my purpose. I accordingly commenced my pedestrian tour on Saturday morning, the 16th September. I set out for Manchester. It was a long but pleasant walk. I well remember, when nearing Manchester, that I sat down to rest for a time on Patricroft Bridge. I was attracted by the rural aspect of the country, and the antique cottages of the neighbourhood. The Bridgewater Canal lay before me, and as I was told that it was the first mile of the waterway that the great Duke had made, it became quite classic ground in my eyes. I little thought at the time that I was so close to a piece of ground that should afterwards become my own, and where I should for twenty years carry on the most active and interesting business of my life.

(*On his walk to London Nasmyth passed through the Black Country and came to Birmingham.*)

I reached the town in the evening, and found most comfortable quarters. On the following day I visited some of the factories where processes were carried on in connection with the Birmingham trade.

I was especially attracted by Soho, once the famous manufacturing establishment of Boulton and Watt. Although this was not the birthplace of the condensing steam-engine, it was the place where it attained its full manhood of efficiency, and became the source and origin of English manufacturing power. Watt's engine has had a greater influence on the productive arts of mankind than any other that can be named. Boulton also was a thorough man of business, without whom, perhaps, Watt could never have made his way against the world, or perfected his magnificent invention. Not less interesting to my mind was the memory of that incomparable mechanic, William Murdoch, a man of indomitable energy, and Watt's right-hand man in the highest practical sense. Murdoch was the inventor of the first model locomotive, and the inventor of gas for lighting purposes; and yet he always kept himself in the background, for he was excessively modest. He was happiest when he could best promote the welfare of the great house of Boulton and Watt. Indeed he was a man whose memory ought to be held in highest regard by all true engineers and mechanics.

The sight which I obtained of the vast series of workshops of this celebrated establishment—filled with evidences of the mechanical genius of these master minds—made me feel that I was indeed on classic ground in regard to everything connected with steam-engine machinery. Some of the engines designed by Watt—the prototypes of the powerful condensing engines of the present day—were still performing their daily quota of work. There was 'Old Bess', a sort of experimental engine upon which Watt had tried many adaptations and alterations for the purpose of suiting it for pumping water from coal mines. There was also the engine with the sun-and-planet motion, an invention of William Murdoch's. Both of these engines were still at work.

When I look back upon that tour I feel that I was amply rewarded. It was throughout delightful and instructive. I came back refreshed for work, and possessed by an anxious desire to press forward in the career of industry which I had set before me to accomplish.

Mr Maudsley arrived from Berlin two days after my return to London. Soon after his return, a very interesting job was brought to him, in which he took even more than his usual interest. It was a machine which his friend Mr Barton, of the Royal Mint, had obtained from France. It was intended to cut or engrave the steel dies used for stamping coin. It was a remarkable and interesting specimen of inventive ingenuity. It copied any object in relief which had been cast in plaster of Paris or brass from the artist's original wax model. The minutest detail was transferred to soft steel dies with absolute accuracy. This remarkable machine could copy and cut steel dies either in intaglio or in cameo of any size, and, in short, enabled the mechanic who managed it to transfer the most minute and characteristic touches of the original model to the steel dies for any variety or size of coin. Nevertheless, the execution of some of the details of the machine was so defective that after giving the most tempting proof of its capabilities at the Royal Mint, Mr Barton found it absolutely necessary to place it in Maudsley's hands, in order to have its details thoroughly overhauled and made as mechanically perfect as its design and intention merited.

This interesting machine was accordingly brought to the private workshop, and placed in the hands of the leading mechanic, James Sherriff, one of our most skilled workmen, with whom I had the pleasure of being associated. We were both put to our mettle. It was a job quite to my taste, and being with so skilled a workman as Sherriff, and in constant communication with Mr Maudsley, I had every opportunity of bringing my best manipulative ability into action and use while perfecting this beautiful machine. It is sufficient to say that by our united efforts, by the technical details suggested by Mr Maudsley and carried out by us, and by the practical trials made under the superintendence of Mr Wyon of the Mint, the apparatus was at length made perfect, and performed its duty to the satisfaction of every one concerned.

Mr Maudsley was a man of a wide range of mechanical

abilities. He was always ready to enter upon any new work requiring the exercise of special skill. It did not matter whether it was machine tools, engraving dies, block machinery, or astronomical instruments. While at Berlin he went to see the Royal Observatory. He was naturally much interested by the fine instruments there—the works of Repsoldt and Mertz, the pioneers of improved astronomical workmanship. The continental instrument-makers were then far in advance of those of England. Mr Maudsley was greatly impressed with the sight of the fine instruments in the Berlin Observatory. He was permitted to observe some of the most striking and remarkable of the heavenly bodies—Jupiter, Saturn and the Moon. It was almost a revelation to him; for the subject was entirely novel. To be able to make such instruments seemed to him to be a glorious achievement of refined mechanism and manipulative skill. He returned home full of the wonderful sights he had seen. It was a constant source of pleasure to him to dwell upon the splendour and magnificence of the heavenly bodies.

He became anxious to possess a powerful telescope of his own. His principal difficulty was in procuring a lens of considerable diameter, possessed of high perfection of defining power. I suggested to him the employment of a reflecting telescope, by means of which the difficulties connected with the employment of glass could be avoided. Mr Maudsley was interested in the idea I suggested, and he requested me to show him what I knew of the art of compounding the alloy called speculum metal. He wished to know how so brittle a material could be cast and ground and polished, and kept free from flaws or defects of every kind.

I accordingly cast for him a speculum of 8 inches diameter. I ground and polished it, and had it fitted up in a temporary manner to exhibit its optical capabilities, which were really of no mean order. But, as his ambition was to have a grand and powerful instrument of not less than 24 inches diameter, the preparation for such a speculum became a subject to him of the highest interest. He began to look out for a proper position for his projected observatory. His mind was full of this idea when he was called away by the claims of affection to visit a dear old friend at Boulogne. But on his return voyage across the Channel he caught a severe cold. On reaching London he took to his bed and never left it alive. After three or four weeks' suffering he died on the 14th of February 1831.

It was a very sad thing for me to lose my dear old master. He was so good and so kind to me in all ways. He treated me like a friend and companion. He was always generous, manly, and upright in his dealings with everybody. How his workmen loved him; how his friends lamented him! He directed, before his death, that he should be buried in Woolwich Churchyard. He had ever a warm heart for Woolwich, where he had been born and brought up. He began his life as a mechanic there, and worked his way steadily upwards until he reached the highest point of his profession. It was natural, therefore, that being so proud of his early connection with Woolwich he should wish his remains to be laid there; and Woolwich, on its part, has equal reason to be proud of Henry Maudsley.

After the death of my master I passed over to the service of his worthy partner, Joshua Field. I had an equal pleasure in working under him. The first work I had to perform for Mr Field was to assist him in making the working drawings of a 200 horse-power condensing steam-engine, ordered by the Lambeth Waterworks Company. The practical acquaintance which I had by this time acquired of the mechanism of steam-engines enabled me to serve Mr Field in a satisfactory manner. I drew out in full practical detail the rough but excellent hand sketches with which he supplied me. They were handed out for execution in the various parts of the factory; and I communicated with the foremen as to the details and work-manship.

While I was occupied beside Mr Field in making these working drawings, he gave me many most valuable hints as to the designing of machinery in general. In after years I had many opportunities of making good use of them. One point he often impressed upon me. It was, he said, most important to bear in mind the *get-at-ability* of parts—that is, when any part of a machine was out of repair, it was requisite to get at it easily without taking the machine to pieces. This may appear a very simple remark, but the neglect of such an arrangement occasions a vast amount of trouble, delay, and expense. None but those who have had to do with the repair of worn-out or damaged parts of machinery can adequately value the importance of this subject.

I found Mr Field to be a most systematic man in all business affairs. I may specially name one of his arrangements which I was quick to take up and appreciate. I carried it out with great advantage in my after life. It was, to record subjects of conversation by means of 'graphic' memoranda. Almost daily, persons of note came to consult with him about machinery. On these occasions the consultations took place either with reference to proposed new work or to the progress of orders then in hand. Sometimes some novel scheme of applying power was under discussion, or some new method of employing mechanism. On ordinary occasions rough and rapid sketches may be made on any stray pieces of waste paper that are about, and after the conversation is over the papers are swept away into the waste basket and destroyed. And yet some of these rapid drawings may involve matters of great interest and importance for after consultations.

To avoid such losses, Mr Field had always placed upon his table a 'talking book' or 'graphic diary'. When his visitors called and entered into conversation with him about mechanical matters, he made rapid sketches on the successive pages of the book, and entered the brief particulars and date of the conversation, together with the name and address of the visitor, so that a conversation, once begun, might again be referred to, and, when the visitor called, the graphic memoranda might be recalled without loss of time, and the consultation again proceed. The pages of Mr Field's 'talking books' were in many ways most interesting. They contained data that in future years supplied valuable evidence in respect to first suggestions of mechanical contrivances, which sometimes were developed into very important results.

CHAPTER VII

I set up in Business: Edinburgh and Manchester

THE completion of the working drawings of the Lambeth pumping engines occupied me until August 1831. I had then arrived at my twenty-third year. I had no intention of proceeding further as an assistant or a journeyman. I intended to begin business for myself. Of course I could only begin in a very small way. I informed Mr Field of my intention, and he was gratified with my decision. Not only so; but he kindly permitted me to obtain castings of one of the best turning-lathes in the workshops. I knew that when I had fitted it up it would become the parent of a vast progeny of descendants—not only in the direct line, but in planing machines, screw-cutting lathes, and many other minor tools.

At the end of the month, after taking a grateful farewell of Mr Field and his partners, I set sail for Leith with my stock of

PLATE III

NASMYTH'S TEMPORARY WORKSHOP AT EDINBURGH

THE FACTORY FLAT AT MANCHESTER

castings, and reached Edinburgh in due time. In order to proceed with the construction of my machine tools, I rented a small piece of land at Old Broughton. It was at the rear of my worthy friend George Douglass's small foundry, and was only about five minutes' walk from my father's house. I erected a temporary workshop 24 feet long by 16 feet wide.

I removed thither my father's foot-lathe, to which I had previously added an excellent slide-rest of my own making. I also added a 'slow motion', which enabled me to turn cast-iron and cast-steel portions of my great Maudsley lathe. I soon had the latter complete and in action. Its first child was a planing machine capable of executing surfaces in the most perfect style —of 3 feet long by 1 foot 8 inches wide. Armed with these two most important and generally useful tools, and with some special additions, such as boring machines and drilling machines, I soon had a progeny of descendants crowded about my little workshop, so that I often did not know which way to turn.

I had one labourer to drive the wheel which gave motion to my big lathe; but I was very much in want of some one else to help me. One day a young hearty fellow called upon me. He had come from the Shotts Iron Company's Works in Edinburgh. Having heard of what I was about, he offered his services. When he told me that he had been bred as a millwright, and that he could handle the plane and the saw as well as the chisel and file, I closed with him at once. He was to have fifteen shillings a week. I liked the young man very much—he was so hearty and cheerful. His name was Archibald Torry, or 'Archie', as he was generally called during the twenty years that he remained in my service.

I obtained another assistant in the person of a young man whose father wished him to get an insight into practical engineering. I was offered a premium of £50 for twelve months' experience in my workshop. I arranged to take the young man, and to initiate him into the general principles and practice of engineering. The £50 premium was a very useful help to me, especially as I had engaged the millwright. It enabled me to pay Torry's wages during the time that he remained with me in Edinburgh. I found it necessary, however, to take in some work in the regular way of business, in order to supply me with the means of completing my proper supply of tools.

The chief of these extraneous and, I may say, disturbing jobs, was that of constructing a rotary steam-engine. Mr Robert Steen had contrived and patented an engine of this sort. He was a dangerously enthusiastic man, and entertained the most visionary ideas as to steam power. He was of opinion that his own contrivance was more compact and simple, and possessed more capability of producing power from the consumption of a given quantity of fuel, than the best steam-engines then in use. I warned him of his error; but nothing but an actual proof would satisfy him. He urgently requested me to execute his order. He made me a liberal and tempting offer of weekly payments for my work during the progress of his engine. He only required that I should give his invention the benefit of my careful workmanship. He considered that this would be sufficient to substantiate all his enthusiastic expectations. I was thus induced to accept his order.

I made the requisite drawings, and proceeded with the work. At the same time my own machine tools were in progress, though at a retarded pace. The weekly payments were regularly made, and I was kept in a sort of financial ease. After three months the rotary engine was finished to the inventor's complete satisfaction. But when the power it gave out was compared with that of a good ordinary steam-engine, the verdict as to consumption of fuel was against the new rotary engine. Nevertheless, the enthusiastic projector ('tho' vanquished he would argue still') insisted that the merits of his contrivance

PLATE IV

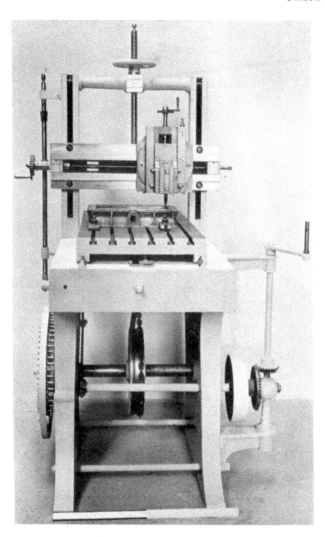

NASMYTH'S FIRST PLANING MACHINE

(By permission, Science Museum, South Kensington)

would sooner or later cause it to be a most formidable rival to the crank steam-engines. As he was pleased with its performances, I had no reason to be dissatisfied. I had done my part in the matter, and Mr Steen had done his. His punctual weekly payments had assisted me in the completion of my tools; and after a few months' more labour I had everything ready for starting business on my own account.

My choice lay between Liverpool and Manchester. I had seen both of these cities while on my visit to Lancashire, and I felt assured that in either of them—the centres of commercial and manipulative energy—I could settle down with my limited capital and tools, and in course of time contrive to get on, helped by energy, self-reliance, and determination. I also found that the demand for machine-making tools was considerable, and that their production would soon become an important department of business. It might be carried on with little expenditure of capital, as the risks were small and the returns were quick. I resolved to cultivate that moderate and safe class of mechanical business, at all events at the outset.

(*Nasmyth visited Liverpool, and later went on to Manchester.*)

I visited John Chippendale, of the firm of Thomson, Chippendale and Company, calico printers. I had met him at a friend's house in London, where he had offered, if I ever visited Manchester, to introduce me to some of the best men there.

Mr Chippendale first introduced me to Mr John Kennedy, one of the most distinguished men in Manchester. I explained to him the object of my visit, and he cordially entered into my views. He left his occupation at the time, and went with me to see a place which he thought might be suitable for my workshop. The building was near at hand—in Dale Street, Piccadilly. It had been used as a cotton mill, but was abandoned by the owner in favour of more suitable and extensive premises.

It was now let out in flats for manufacturing purposes. Power was supplied to each flat from a shaft connected with a large mill up the street, the owner of which had power to spare. The flat shown to me was 130 feet long by 27 feet wide, and the rent was only £50 a year. I thought the premises very suitable, but I took a night to sleep over it. I thanked Mr Kennedy very much for his kindness, and for the trouble which he had taken on behalf of an unknown stranger.

On this memorable day I had another introduction, through the kindness of Mr Chippendale, which proved of great service to me. It was to the Messrs Grant, the famous 'Brothers Cheeryble' of Dickens. I was taken to their counting-house in Cannon Street, where I was introduced to Daniel Grant. Although business was at its full height, he gave me a cordial reception. But, to save time, he invited me to come after the Exchange was over and take 'tiffin' with him at his hospitable mansion in Moseley Street. There, he said, I should meet some of the most enterprising men in Lancashire. I was most happy, of course, to avail myself of his invitation. I went thither accordingly, and the first thing that Daniel did was to present me in the most cordial manner to 'his noble brother William', as he always affectionately called him. William was the head of the firm, and he, too, gave me a warm and hearty welcome. He asked me to sit beside him at the head of the table.

During dinner—for indeed it was such, being the survival of the old-fashioned one o'clock dinner of a departing age— William entered into conversation with me. He took occasion to inquire into the object of my visit to Manchester. I told him, as briefly as I could, that I intended to begin the business of a mechanical engineer on a very moderate scale, and that I had been looking out for premises wherein to commence operations. He seemed interested, and asked more questions. I related to him my little history, and told him of my desires, hopes, and

aspirations. 'What was my age?' 'Twenty-six.' 'That is a very
young age at which to begin business on your own account.'
'Yes; but I have plenty of work in me, and I am very economical.' Then he pressed his questions home. 'But what is your
capital?' I told him that my capital in cash was £63. 'What!'
he said, 'that will do very little for you when Saturday nights
come round.' 'That's true,' I answered; 'but as there will be
only myself and Archie Torry to provide for, I think I can
manage to get along very well until profitable work comes in.'

He whispered to me, 'Keep your heart up!' With such
views, he said, I was sure to do well. And if, he added, on any
Saturday night I wanted money to pay wages or other expenses,
I would find a credit for £500 at 3 per cent. at his office in
Cannon Street, 'and no security'. These were his very words.
What could have been more generous? I could only whisper
my earnest thanks for his warm-hearted kindness. He gave me
a kindly squeeze of the hand in return, which set me in a glow
of gladness. He also gave me a sort of wink that I shall never
forget—a most knowing wink. In looking at me he seemed to
turn his eye round and brought his eyebrows down upon it in a
sudden and extraordinary manner. I thought it was a mere
confirmation of his kind advice to 'keep my heart up!' It was
not until two years after I found, from a mutual friend, that the
eye in question was *made of glass*! Sometimes the glass eye got
slightly out of its place, and Mr Grant had to force it in again
by this odd contortion of his eyebrows, which I had translated
into all manner of kind intentions.

As soon as the party broke up I went to Wren and Bennett,
the agents for the flat of the old mill which I had seen in Dale
Street. I inspected it again, and found that it was in all respects
suitable for my purpose. I may mention in passing that the
flat below mine was in the occupation of a glass-cutter, whose
glass-cutting lathes and grindstones were supplied with power

from the same upright shaft that was to serve me in the same manner on the flat above. Encouraged by the support of William Grant, I immediately entered into a contract for the premises as a yearly tenant. Nothing could have been more happily arranged for my entering into business as a mechanical engineer and machine-tool maker. The situation of the premises was excellent, being in the heart of Manchester.

When I had settled the contract for taking the place, I wrote to Edinburgh by that night's post to tell my father of the happy result of my visit to Manchester, and also to inform my right-hand man, Archie Torry, that I should soon be with him. He was to prepare for packing up my lathes, planing machines, drilling machines, and other smaller tools, not forgetting my father's foot-lathe, of which I had made such effective use. I soon followed up my letter. I was in Edinburgh in a few days' time, and had all my tools packed up. In the course of about ten days I returned to Manchester, and was followed by Archie Torry and the ponderous cases of machinery and engineer's tools. They were all duly delivered, hoisted to my flat, and put in their proper places. I was then ready for work.

The very first order I received was from my friend Edward Tootal. It was a new metallic piston for the small steam-engine that gave motion to his silk-winding machinery. It was necessary that it should be done over-night, in order that his factory should be at work as usual in the morning. My faithful Archie and I set to work accordingly. We removed the old defective piston, and replaced it by a new and improved one, made according to my own ideas of how so important a part of a steam-engine should be constructed. We conveyed it to Mr Tootal's factory over-night, and by five o'clock in the morning gave it a preliminary trial to see that everything was in order. The 'hands' came in at six, and the machine was set to work. It was no doubt a very small order, but the piston was executed perfectly and satisfactorily. The result of its easier action, through reduced friction, was soon observable in the smaller consumption of coal. Mr Tootal and his brother were highly pleased at my prompt and careful attention to their little order, and it was the forerunner of better things to come.

Orders soon came in. My planing machine was soon fully occupied. When not engaged in executing other work it was employed in planing the flat cast-iron inking tables for printing machines, which were made in considerable numbers by Messrs Wren and Bennett, my landlords. I had many small subsidiary jobs sent to me to execute. They not only served to keep my machine tools properly employed, but tended in the most effective way to make my work known to some of the best firms in Manchester, who in course of time became my employers.

In order to keep pace with the influx of work I had to take on fresh hands. I established a smithy down in the cellar flat of the old mill in Dale Street, so that all forge work in iron and steel might be promptly and economically produced on the premises. There was a small iron-foundry belonging to a Mr Heath, about three minutes' walk from my workshop, where I had all my castings of iron and brass done with promptness, and of excellent quality. Mr Heath very much wanted a more powerful steam-engine to drive his cupola blowing fan. I had made a steam-engine in Edinburgh and brought it with me. There it lay in my workshop, where it remained unused, for I was sufficiently supplied with power from the rotating shaft. Mr Heath offered to buy it. The engine was accordingly removed to his iron-foundry, and I received my full quota of value in castings.

Week by week my orders grew, and the flat of the old mill soon assumed a very busy aspect. By occasionally adding to the number of my lathes, drilling machines, and other engineer's tools, I attracted the attention of employers. When seen in action they not only facilitated and economised the production of my own work, but became my best advertisements. Each new tool that I constructed had some feature of novelty about it. I always endeavoured after greater simplicity and perfectness of workmanship. I was punctual in all my engagements. The business proved safe and profitable. The returns were quick. Sometimes one-third of the money was paid in advance on receipt of the order, and the balance was paid on delivery at my own premises. All risk of bad debts was avoided. Thus I was enabled to carry on my business with a very moderate amount of capital.

My business went on prosperously. I had plenty of orders, and did my best to execute them satisfactorily. Shortly after the opening of the Liverpool and Manchester Railway there was a largely increased demand for machine-making tools. The success of that line led to the construction of other lines, concentrating in Manchester; and every branch of manufacture shared in the prosperity of the time.

Most of my own machine tools were self-acting—planing machines, slide lathes, drilling, boring, slotting machines, and so on. When set up in my workshop they distinguished themselves by their respective merits and efficiency. They were, in fact, their own best advertisements. The consequence was that orders for similar machines poured in upon me, and the floor of my flat became completely loaded with the work in hand.

The tenant below me, it will be remembered, was a glass-cutter. He observed, with alarm, the bits of plaster from the roof coming down among his cut glasses and decanters. He thought that the rafters overhead were giving way, and that the whole of my machinery and engines would come tumbling down upon him some day and involve him in ruin. He probably exaggerated the danger; still there was some cause for fear.

When the massive castings on my floor were moved about from one part to another, the floor quivered and trembled under the pressure. The glass-cutter complained to the landlord, and the landlord expostulated with me. I did all that I could to equalise the pressure, and prevent vibration as much as possible. But at length, in spite of all my care, an accident occurred which compelled me to take measures to remove my machinery to other premises. As this removal was followed by consequences of much importance to myself, I must endeavour to state the circumstances under which it occurred.

My kind friend John Kennedy continued to take the greatest interest in my welfare. It was through his influence that I obtained an order for a high-pressure steam-engine of twenty horse-power to drive the machinery connected with a distillery at Londonderry, in Ireland. I was afraid at first that I could not undertake the job. The size of the engine was somewhat above the height of my flat and it would probably occupy too much space in my already overcrowded workshop. At the same time I was most anxious not to let such an order pass me. I wished to please my friend Mr Kennedy; besides, the execution of the engine might lead to further business.

At length, after consideration, I undertook to execute the order. Instead of constructing the engine perpendicularly, I constructed it lying upon its side. There was a little extra difficulty, but I managed to complete it in the best style. It had next to be taken to pieces for the purpose of being conveyed to Londonderry. It was then that the accident happened. My men had the misfortune to allow the end of the engine beam to crash through the floor! There was a terrible scattering of lath and plaster and dust. The glass-cutter was in a dreadful state. He rushed forthwith to the landlord, and called upon him to come at once and *judge for himself*!

Mr Wren *did* come, and *did* judge for himself. He looked in at the glass shop, and saw the damage that had been done amongst the tumblers and decanters. There was the hole in the roof, through which the end of the engine beam had come and scattered the lath and plaster. The landlord then came to me. The whole flat was filled with machinery, including the steam-engine on its side, now being taken to pieces for the purpose of shipment to Ireland. Mr Wren, in the kindest manner, begged me to remove from the premises as soon as I could, otherwise the whole building might be brought to the ground with the weight of my machinery. 'Besides,' he argued, 'you must have more convenient premises for your rapidly extending business.' It was quite true. I must leave the place and establish myself elsewhere.

CHAPTER VIII

Patricroft: The Bridgewater Foundry

THE reader may remember that while on my journey on foot from Liverpool to Manchester in 1830, I had rested myself for a little on the parapet of the bridge overlooking the canal near Patricroft, and gazed longingly upon a plot of land situated along the canal side. On the afternoon of the day on which the engine beam crashed through the glass-cutter's roof, I went out again to look at that favourite piece of land. There it was, unoccupied, just as I had seen it some years before. I went to it and took note of its dimensions. It consisted of about six acres. It was covered with turf, and as flat and neat as a bowling-green. It was bounded on one side by the Bridgewater Canal, edged by a neat stone margin 1050 feet long, on another side by the Liverpool and Manchester Railway, while on a third side it was bounded by a good road, accessible from all sides. The plot was splendidly situated. I wondered that it had not been secured before. It was evidently waiting for me!

I did not allow the grass to grow beneath my feet. That very night I ascertained that the proprietor of this most beautiful plot was Squire Trafford, one of the largest landed proprietors in the district. Next morning I proceeded to Trafford Hall for the purpose of interviewing the Squire. He received me most cordially. After I had stated my object in calling upon him, he said he would be exceedingly pleased to have me for one of his tenants. He gave me a letter of introduction to his agent, Mr Thomas Lee, of Princes Street, Manchester, with whom I was to arrange as to the terms. I was offered a lease of the six-acre plot for 999 years, at an annual rental of $1\frac{3}{4}d$. per square yard. This proposal was most favourable, as I obtained the advantage of a fee-simple purchase without having to sink capital in the land. All that I had to provide for was the annual rent.

My next step in this important affair was to submit the proposal to the judgment of my excellent friend Edward Lloyd, the banker. He advised me to close the matter as soon as possible, for he too considered the terms most favourable. Within a few days the lease was signed and I was in possession of the land upon which the Bridgewater Foundry was afterwards erected.[1]

As soon as the preliminary arrangements for the lease of the six-acre plot had been made, I proceeded to make working drawings of a temporary timber workshop; as I was anxious to unload the floor of my flat in Dale Street, and to get as much

---

[1] I called the place the Bridgewater Foundry as an appropriate and humble tribute to the memory of the first great canal-maker in Britain—the noble Duke of Bridgewater. My ground was on the first mile of the Bridgewater Canal which the Duke had constructed under the superintendence of Brindley, so that it might well be considered, in an engineering sense, 'classic ground'.

of my machinery as possible speedily removed to Patricroft. For the purpose of providing the temporary accommodation, I went to Liverpool and purchased a number of logs of New Brunswick pine. The logs were cut up into planks, battens, and roof-timbers, and were delivered in a few days at the canal wharf in front of my plot. The building of the workshops rapidly proceeded. By the aid of some handy active carpenters, super-intended by my energetic foreman, Archie Torry, several convenient well-lighted workshops were soon ready for the reception of my machinery. I had a four horse-power engine, which I had made at Edinburgh, ready to be placed in position, together with the boiler. This was the first power I employed in starting my new works.

I must return for a moment to the twenty horse-power engine, which had been the proximate cause of my removal from Dale Street. It was taken to pieces, packed, and sent off to Londonderry. When I was informed that it was erected and ready for work I proceeded to Ireland to see it begin its operations.

I may briefly say that the engine gave every satisfaction, and I believe that it continues working to this day. I had the pleasure of bringing back with me an order for a condensing engine of forty horse-power, required by Mr John Munn for giving motion to his new flax mill, then under construction. I mention this order because the engine was the first important piece of work executed at the Bridgewater Foundry.

I returned to Patricroft, and found the wooden workshops nearly finished. The machine tools were, for the most part, fixed and ready for use. In August 1836 the Bridgewater Foundry was in complete and efficient action. The engine ordered at Londonderry was at once put in hand, and the concern was fairly started in its long career of prosperity. The wooden workshops had been erected upon the grass. But the sward soon disappeared. The hum of the driving belts, the whirl of the machinery, the sound of the hammer upon the anvil, gave the place an air of busy activity. As work increased, workmen increased. The workshops were enlarged. Wood gave place to brick. Cottages for the accommodation of the work-people sprang up in the neighbourhood; and what had once been quiet grassy fields became the centre of a busy population.

(*Lord Francis Egerton lived at Worsley Hall, near the Foundry. He had some friendly dealings with Nasmyth concerning the use of a canal wharf on his property.*)

Lord Francis Egerton, soon after created Earl of Ellesmere, became one of the most constant visitors to the foundry, in which he always took a lively interest. He delighted to go through the workshops, and enjoy the sight of the active machinery and the work in progress. One of his favourite sights was the pouring out of the molten iron into moulds for the larger class of castings; when some twelve or sixteen tons, by the aid of my screw safety ladle, were decanted with as much neatness and exactness as the pouring out of a glass of wine from a decanter.

I must here say a few words as to my screw safety ladle. I had observed the great danger occasioned to workmen by the method of emptying the molten iron into the casting moulds. The white-hot fluid was run from the melting furnace into a large ladle with one or two cross handles and levers, worked by a dozen or fifteen men. The ladle contained many tons of molten iron, and was transferred by a crane to the moulds. To do this required the greatest caution and steadiness. If a stumble took place, and the ladle was in the slightest degree upset, there was splash of hot metal on the floor, which, in the recoil, flew against the men's clothes, set them on fire, or occasioned frightful scalds and burns.

Old Type of Foundry Ladle

Nasmyth's Safety Foundry Ladle

To prevent these accidents I invented my safety foundry ladle. I applied a screw wheel, keyed to the trunnion of the ladle, which was acted on by an endless screw attached to the sling of the ladle; and by this means one man could move the largest ladle on its axis, and pour out its molten contents with the most perfect ease and safety. Not only was all risk of accident thus removed, but the perfection of the casting was secured by the steady continuous flow of the white-hot metal into the mould. The nervous anxiety and confusion that usually attended the pouring of the metal required for the larger class of castings was thus entirely avoided.

I had no difficulty in obtaining abundance of skilled workmen in South Lancashire and Cheshire. I was in the neighbourhood of Manchester, which forms the centre of a population gifted with mechanical instinct. From an early period the finest sort of mechanical work has been turned out in that part of England. Much of the talent is inherited. It descends from father to son, and develops itself from generation to generation. I may mention one curious circumstance connected with the pedigree of Manchester; that much of the mechanical excellence of its workmen descends from the Norman smiths and armourers introduced into the neighbourhood at the Norman Conquest by Hugo de Lupus, the chief armourer of William the Conqueror, after the battle of Hastings, in 1066.

I was first informed of this circumstance by William Stubbs of Warrington, then maker of the celebrated 'Lancashire files'. The 'P.S.', or Peter Stubbs's files, were so vastly superior to other files, both in the superiority of the steel and in the perfection of the cutting, which long retained its efficiency, that every workman gloried in the possession and use of such durable tools. Being naturally interested in everything connected with tools and mechanics, I was exceedingly anxious to visit the factory where these admirable files were made. I obtained an introduction to William Stubbs, then head of the firm, and was received by him with much cordiality. When I asked him if I might be favoured with a sight of his factory, he replied that he had no factory, as such; and that all he had to do in supplying his large warehouse was to serve out the requisite quantities of pure cast steel as rods and bars to the workmen; and that they, on their part, forged the metal into files of every description at their own cottage workshops, principally situated in the neighbouring counties of Cheshire and Lancashire.

This information surprised as well as pleased me. Mr Stubbs proceeded to give me an account of the origin of this peculiar system of cottage manufacture in his neighbourhood. It appears that Hugo de Lupus, William the Conqueror's Master of Arms, the first Earl of Chester, settled in North Cheshire shortly after the Conquest. He occupied Halton Castle, and his workmen resided in Warrington and the adjacent villages of Appleton, Widnes, Prescot, and Cuerdley. There they produced coats of steel, mail armour, and steel and iron weapons under the direct superintendence of their chief.

The manufacture thus founded continued for many centuries. Although the use of armour was discontinued, these workers in steel and iron still continued famous. The skill that had formerly been employed in forging chain armour and war instruments was devoted to more peaceful purposes. The cottage workmen made the best of files and steel tools of other kinds. Their talent became hereditary, and the manufacture of wire in all its forms is almost peculiar to Warrington and the neighbourhood. Mr Stubbs also informed me that most of the workmen's peculiar names for tools and implements were traceable to old Norman-French words.

To return to my narrative. In the midst of such a habitually industrious population, it will be obvious that there was no difficulty in finding a sufficient supply of able workmen. It was

PLATE V

BRIDGEWATER FOUNDRY IN 1838

(After a painting by Alexander Nasmyth)

for the most part the most steady, respectable, and well-conducted classes of mechanics who sought my employment—not only for the good wages they received, but for the sake of their own health and that of their families; for it will be remembered that the foundry and the workmen's dwellings were surrounded by the fresh, free, open country. In the course of a few years the locality became a thriving colony of skilled mechanics. In order to add to the accommodation of the increasing numbers, an additional portion of land, amounting to eight acres, was leased from Squire Trafford on the same terms as before. On this land suitable houses and cottages for the foremen and workmen were erected. At the same time substantial brick workshops were built in accordance with my original general plan, to meet the requirements of our rapidly expanding business, until at length a large and commodious factory was erected.

I desire to say a few words about those excellent helpers, the foremen engineers, who zealously helped me in my undertaking from beginning to end.

I must place my most worthy, zealous, and faithful Archie Torry at the top of the list. He rose from being my only workman when I first started in Manchester, to be my chief general foreman. The energy and devotion which he brought to bear upon my interests set a high example to all in my employment. His hearty zeal and cheerful temper, and his energetic movement when among the men, had a sympathetic influence upon all about him. We were often called in by our neighbour manufacturers to repair a breakdown of their engines. That was always a sad disaster, as all hands were idle until the repair was effected. Archie was in his glory on such occasions. By his ready zeal and energy he soon got over the difficulty, repaired the engines and set the people to work again. He became quite famous in these cases of extreme urgency. He never spared himself, and his example had an excellent effect upon every workman under him.

Another of my favourite workshop lieutenants was James Hutton. He had been leading foreman to my worthy friend George Douglass, of Old Broughton, Edinburgh. After I left Edinburgh he had emigrated to the United States for the purpose of bettering his condition. Shortly after my removal to Patricroft, and when everything had been got into full working order, I received a letter from him in which he said that he was anxious to return to England, and asking if there was any vacancy in our establishment that he might be employed to fill up. It so happened that the foremanship of turners was then vacant. I informed Hutton of the post; and on his return to England he was duly enrolled in our staff.

The situation was a very important one, and Hutton filled it admirably. He was a sound practical man, and thoroughly knew every department of engineering mechanism. As I had provided small separate rooms or offices for every department of the establishment for the use of the foremen, where they kept their memoranda and special tools, I had often the pleasure of conferring with Hutton as to some point of interest, or when I wished to pass my ideas and designs through the ordeal of his judgment, in order that I might find out any lurking defect in some proposed mechanical arrangement. Before he gave an opinion, Hutton always took a pinch of snuff to stimulate his intellect, or rather to give him a little time for consideration. He would turn the subject over in his mind. But I knew that I could trust his keenness of insight. He would give his verdict carefully, shrewdly, and truthfully. Hutton remained a faithful and valued servant in the concern for nearly thirty years, and died at a ripe old age.

Another of my excellent assistants was John Clerk. He was a most able man in some of the more important branches of

mechanical engineering. He had, besides, an excellent knowledge of building operations. I found him of great use in
superintending the erection of the additional workshops which
were required as our business extended. He made out full-
sized chalk-line drawings from my original pencil sketches,
on the large floor of the pattern store, and from these were
formed the working drawings for the new buildings. He had
a wonderful power of rapidity and clearness in apprehend-
ing new subjects, and the way in which he depicted them in
large drawings was quite masterly. John Clerk and I spent
many an hour on our knees together on the pattern store floor,
and the result of our deliberations usually was some substantial
addition to the workshops of the foundry, or some extra large
and powerful machine-tool.

The last of our foremen to whom I shall refer was worthy
Thomas Crewdson. He entered our service as a smith, in which
pursuit he displayed great skill. We soon noted the high order
of his natural ability; promoted him from the ranks, and made
him the foreman of the smith's and forge-work department. In
this he displayed every quality of excellence, not only in seeing
to the turning out of the forge work in the highest state of
perfection, but in managing the men under his charge with
such kind discretion as to maintain the most perfect harmony
in the workshops. This is always a matter of great importance—
that the foreman should inspire the workmen with his own
spirit, and keep up their harmony and activity to the most
productive point. Crewdson was so systematic in his use of time
that we found that he was able also to undertake the foremanship of the boiler-making department, in addition to that of the
smith work; and to this he was afterwards appointed, with highly
satisfactory results to all concerned.

So strongly and clearly impressed is my mind with the
recollection of the valuable assistance which I received during

my engineering life from these vicegerents of practical management at Patricroft, that I feel that I cannot proceed further in
my narrative without thus placing the merits of these worthy
men upon record. It was a source of great good fortune to me
to be associated with them, and I consider them to have been
among the most important elements in the prosperity of the
Bridgewater Foundry.

CHAPTER IX

Locomotive Building: The Birth of the Steam Hammer

I WAS present at the opening of the Liverpool and Manchester
Railway, on the 15th of September 1830. Everyone knows the
success of the undertaking. Railways became the rage. They
were projected in every possible direction.

They were first made between all the large towns, after
which branches were constructed to place the whole country in
connection with the main lines. Coaches were driven off the
road, and everything appeared to be thrown into a state of
confusion. People wondered greatly at the new conditions of
travelling; and they flocked from all quarters to see the railway
at work.

When the line was opened from Edinburgh to Glasgow a
shepherd and his wife came from beyond the Pentlands to see
the train pass. On it came, and flashed out of sight in a minute.
'How wonderful are the works o' man!' exclaimed the shepherd. 'But *what's a' the hurry for*?' rejoined his wife. Still more
marvellous, however, was the first adventure by train of an old
woman from Newtyle to Dundee. In those days the train was
let down part of the railway by rope. The woman was on her

way down hill, with a basket of eggs by her side. Suddenly the rope broke, and the train dashed into the Dundee Station scattering the carriages, and throwing out the old woman and her basket of broken eggs. A porter ran to her help, when, gathering herself together, she exclaimed, 'Odd sake, sirs, *d'ye aye whummil*[1] *us oot this way?*' She thought it was only the ordinary way of delivering railway passengers.

Ropes, however, were merely exceptional methods of working railway trains. Eventually locomotives were invariably adopted. When railways were extended in so many directions, more and more locomotives were required to work them.

When George Stephenson was engaged in building his first locomotive at Killingworth, he was greatly hampered, not only by the want of handy mechanics, but by the want of efficient tools. But he did the best that he could. His genius overcame difficulties. It was immensely to his credit that he should have so successfully completed his engines for the Stockton and Darlington, and afterwards for the Liverpool and Manchester Railway.

Only a few years had passed, and self-acting tools were now enabled to complete, with precision and uniformity, machines that before had been deemed almost impracticable. In proportion to the rapid extension of railways the demand for locomotives became very great. As our machine tools were peculiarly adapted for turning out a large amount of first-class work, we directed our attention to this class of business. In the course of about ten years after the opening of the Liverpool and Manchester Railway, we executed considerable orders for locomotives for the London and Southampton, the Manchester and Leeds, and the Gloucester railway companies.

The Great Western Railway Company invited us to tender for twenty of their very ponderous engines. They proposed a

[1] WHUMMIL, to turn upside down.—*Jamieson's Scottish Dictionary*.

very tempting condition of the contract. It was, that if, after a month's trial of the locomotives, their working proved satisfactory, a premium of £100 was to be added to the price of each engine and tender. The locomotives were made and delivered; they ran the stipulated number of test miles between London and Bristol in a perfectly satisfactory manner; and we not only received the premium, but, what was much more encouraging, we received a special letter from the Board of Directors, stating their entire satisfaction with the performance of our engines, and desiring us to refer other contractors to them with respect to the excellence of our workmanship. This testimonial was altogether spontaneous, and proved extremely valuable in other quarters.

I may mention that, in order to effect the prompt and perfect execution of this order, I contrived several special machine tools, which assisted us most materially. These tools for the most part rendered us more independent of mere manual strength and dexterity, while at the same time they increased the accuracy and perfection of the work. They afterwards assisted us in perfecting the production of other classes of work.

My connection with the Great Western Company shortly led to a most important event in connection with my own personal history. It appears that their famous steamship the *Great Western* had been very successful in her voyages between Bristol and New York; so much so, indeed, that the directors of the Company ordered the construction of another vessel of much greater magnitude—the *Great Britain*. Mr Francis Humphries, their engineer, came to Patricroft to consult with me as to the machine tools, of unusual size and power, which were required for the construction of the immense engines of the proposed ship, which were to be made on the vertical trunk principle. Very complete works were erected at Bristol for the accommodation of the requisite machinery. The tools were made according to Mr Humphries' order; they were delivered and fitted to his entire approval, and the construction of the gigantic engines was soon in full progress.

An unexpected difficulty, however, was encountered with respect to the enormous wrought-iron intermediate paddle-shaft. It was required to be of a size and diameter the like of which had never been forged. Mr Humphries applied to the largest forges throughout the country for tenders for the price at which they would execute this important part of the work, but to his surprise and dismay he found that not one of them could undertake so large a forging. In this dilemma he wrote a letter to me, which I received on the 24th of November 1839, informing me of the unlooked-for difficulty. 'I find', he said, 'that there is not a forge hammer in England or Scotland powerful enough to forge the intermediate paddle-shaft of the engines for the *Great Britain*! What am I to do? Do you think I might dare to use cast-iron?'

This letter immediately set me a-thinking. How was it that the existing hammers were incapable of forging a wrought-iron shaft of thirty inches diameter? Simply because of their want of compass, of range and fall, as well as of their want of power of blow. A few moments' rapid thought satisfied me that it was by our rigidly adhering to the old traditional form of a smith's hand hammer—of which the forge and tilt hammer, although driven by water or steam power, were merely enlarged modifications—that the difficulty had arisen; as, whenever the largest forge hammer was tilted up to its full height, its range was so small that when a piece of work of considerable size was placed on the anvil, the hammer became 'gagged'; so that, when the forging required the most powerful blow, it received next to no blow at all, as the clear space for the fall of the hammer was almost entirely occupied by the work on the anvil.

The obvious remedy was to contrive some method by which

a ponderous block of iron should be lifted to a sufficient height above the object on which it was desired to strike a blow, and then to let the block fall down upon the forging, guiding it in its descent by such simple means as should give the required precision in the percussive action of the falling mass. Following up this idea, I got out my 'Scheme Book', on the pages of which I generally *thought out*, with the aid of pen and pencil, such mechanical devices as I had conceived in my mind, and was thereby enabled to render them visible. I then rapidly sketched out my Steam Hammer, having it all clearly before me in my mind's eye. In little more than half an hour after receiving Mr Humphries' letter narrating his unlooked-for difficulty, I had the whole contrivance in all its details before me in a page of my Scheme Book. The date of this first drawing was the 24th November 1839.

My Steam Hammer as thus first sketched, consisted of, first, a massive anvil on which to rest the work; second, a block of iron constituting the hammer or blow-giving portion; and, third, an inverted steam cylinder to whose piston-rod the hammer-block was attached. All that was then required to produce a most effective hammer was simply to admit steam of sufficient pressure into the cylinder so as to act on the under-side of the piston, and thus to raise the hammer-block attached to the end of the piston-rod. By a very simple arrangement of a slide valve, under the control of an attendant the steam was allowed to escape and thus permit the massive block of iron rapidly to descend by its own gravity upon the work then upon the anvil.

Thus, by the more or less rapid manner in which the attendant allowed the steam to enter or escape from the cylinder, any required number or any intensity of blows could be delivered. Their succession might be modified in an instant. The hammer might be arrested and suspended according to the requirements

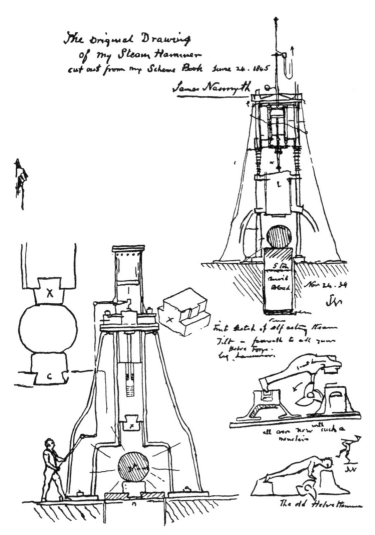

Nasmyth's First Sketch of the Steam Hammer, 1839
From his 'Scheme Book'

of the work. The workman might thus, as it were, *think in blows*. He might deal them out on to the ponderous glowing mass, and mould or knead it into the desired form as if it were a lump of clay; or pat it with gentle taps according to his will, or at the desire of the forgeman.

Rude and rapidly sketched out as it was, this, my first delineation of the steam hammer, will be found to comprise all the essential elements of the invention. Every detail of the drawing retains to this day the form and arrangement which I gave to it forty-three years ago. I believed that the steam hammer would prove practically successful; and I looked forward to its general employment in the forging of heavy masses of iron. It is no small gratification to me now, when I look over my rude and hasty first sketch, to find that I hit the mark so exactly, not only in the general structure but in the details; and that the invention as I then conceived it and put it into shape, still retains its form and arrangements intact in the thousands of steam hammers that are now doing good service in the mechanical arts throughout the civilised world.

But to return to my correspondence with the Great Western Company. I wrote at once to Mr Humphries, and sent him a sketch of my proposed steam hammer. I told him that I felt assured he would now be able to overcome his difficulty, and that the paddle-shaft of the *Great Britain* might now be forged. Mr Humphries was delighted with my design. He submitted it to Mr Brunel, engineer-in-chief of the steamship, and to other persons interested in the undertaking—by all of whom it was heartily approved. I accordingly gave the Company permission to communicate my design to such forge proprietors as might feel disposed to erect the steam hammer, the only condition that I made being that in the event of its being adopted I was to be allowed to supply it in accordance with my design.

But the paddle-shaft of the *Great Britain* was never forged. About that time the substitution of the screw for the paddle-wheel as a means of propulsion was attracting much attention. The performances of the *Archimedes*, as arranged by Mr Francis P. Smith, were so satisfactory that Mr Brunel, after he had made an excursion in that vessel, recommended the directors to adopt the new propelling power. After much discussion, they yielded to his strongly-urged advice. The consequence was that the great engines which Mr Humphries had so elaborately designed, and which were far advanced in construction, were given up, to his inexpressible regret and mortification, as he had pinned his highest hopes as a practical engineer on the results of their performance. There was thus, for a time, an end of the steam hammer required for forging the paddle-shaft of the *Great Britain.*

Very bad times for the iron-trade, and for all mechanical undertakings, set in about this time. A widespread depression affected all conditions of industry. Although I wrote to the heads of all the great firms, urging the importance of my invention, and forwarding designs of my steam hammer, I was unable to obtain a single order. It is true, they cordially approved of my plan, and were greatly struck by its simplicity, unity, and apparent power. But the substance of their replies was that they had not sufficient orders to keep the forge hammers they already possessed in work. They promised, however, that in the event of trade recovering from its depression, they would probably adopt the new power.

In the meantime my invention was taken up in an entirely new and unexpected quarter. I had for some years been supplying foreign customers with self-acting machine tools. The principals of continental manufacturing establishments were accustomed to make frequent visits to England for the purpose of purchasing various machine tools required for the production of the ponderous as well as the lighter parts of their machinery. We gave our foreign visitors every facility and opportunity for seeing our own tools at work, and they were often so much pleased that, when they came to order one special tool, they ended by ordering many—the machine tools in full activity thus acting as their most effective advertisements.

In like manner I freely opened my Scheme Book to any foreign visitors. There I let them see the mechanical thoughts that were passing through my mind, reduced to pen and ink drawings. I did not hesitate to advocate the advantage of my steam hammer over every other method of forging heavy masses of iron; and I pointed out the drawing in my Scheme Book in confirmation of my views. The book was kept in the office to be handy for such occasions; and in many cases it was the means of suggesting ideas of machine tools to our customers, and thus led to orders which might not have been obtained without this effective method of prompting them. Amongst our foreign visitors was M. Schneider, proprietor of the great ironworks at Creuzot, in France. We had supplied him with various machine tools, and he was so pleased with their action that the next time he came to England he called at our office at Patricroft. M. Bourdon, his mechanical manager, accompanied him.

I happened to be absent on a journey at the time; but my partner, Mr Gaskell, was present. After showing them over the works, as an act of courtesy he brought them my Scheme Book and allowed them to examine it. He pointed out the drawing of my Steam Hammer, and told them the purpose for which it was intended. They were impressed with its simplicity and apparent practical utility—so much so, that M. Bourdon took careful notes and sketches of the constructive details of the hammer.

I was informed on my return of the visit of MM. Schneider and Bourdon, but the circumstances of their having inspected the designs in my Scheme Book, and especially my original design of the steam hammer, was regarded by my partner as too ordinary and trivial an incident of their visit to be mentioned to me. The exhibition of my mechanical designs to visitors at the Foundry was a matter of almost daily occurrence. I was, therefore, in entire ignorance of the fact that these foreign visitors had taken with them to France a copy of the plan and details of my steam hammer.

It was not until my visit to France in April 1842 that the upshot of their visit was brought under my notice in an extraordinary manner. I was requested by M. Bouchier, Minister of Marine, to visit the French dockyards and arsenals for the purpose of conferring with the director of each with reference to the supply of various machine tools for the proper equipment of the marine-engine factories in connection with the Royal Dockyards. In order to render this journey more effective and instructive, I visited most of the French engineering establishments which had been supplied with machine tools by our firm. Amongst these was of course the famous firm of Schneider, whose works at Creuzot lay not far out of the way of my return journey. I accordingly made my way thither, and found M. Bourdon at his post, though M. Schneider was absent.

M. Bourdon received me with much cordiality. As he spoke English with fluency I was fortunate in finding him present, in order to show me over the works; on entering which, one of the things that particularly struck me was the excellence of a large wrought-iron marine engine single crank, forged with a remarkable degree of exactness in its general form. I observed also that the large eye of the crank had been punched and drifted with extraordinary smoothness and truth. I inquired of M. Bourdon how that crank had been forged. His immediate reply was, '*It was forged by your steam hammer!*'

Great was my surprise and pleasure at hearing this statement.

I asked him how he had come to be acquainted with my steam hammer. He then narrated the circumstance of his visit to the Bridgewater Foundry during my absence. He told me of my partner having exhibited to him the original design, and how much he was struck by its simplicity and probable efficiency; that he had taken careful notes and sketches on the spot; that among the first things he did after his return to Creuzot was to put in hand the necessary work for the erection of a steam hammer; and that the results had in all respects realised the high expectations he had formed of it.

M. Bourdon conducted me to the forge department of the works, that I might, as he said, '*see my own child*'; and there it was, in truth—thumping child of my brain. Until then it had only existed in my scheme book; and yet it had often and often been before my mind's eye in full action. On inspecting the steam hammer I found that Bourdon had omitted some important details, which had led to a few mishaps, especially with respect to the frequent breaking of the piston-rod at its junction with the hammer block. He had effected this, in the usual way, by means of a wedge through the rod; but he told me that it often broke through the severe jar during the action of the hammer. I sketched for him, then and there, in full size on a board, the elastic packing under the end of the piston-rod, which acted, as I told him, like the cartilage between the bones of the vertebræ, preventing the destructive effects of violent jars. I also communicated to him a few other important details, which he had missed in his hasty inspection of my design. He expressed his obligation to me in the warmest terms, and the alterations which he shortly afterwards effected in the steam hammer, in accordance with my plans, enabled it to accomplish everything that he could desire.

I had not yet taken out a patent for the steam hammer. The reason was this. The cost of a patent at the time I invented it was little short of £500, all expenses included. My partner was unwilling to lay out so large a sum upon an invention for which there seemed to be so little demand at that time; and I myself had the whole of my capital embarked in the concern. I had been warned of the risk I ran by freely exhibiting my original design, as well as by sending drawings of it to those whom I thought were most likely to bring the invention into use. But nothing had as yet been done in England. It was left for France, as I have described, to embody my invention in an actual steam hammer.

I now became alarmed, and feared lest I should lose the benefits of my invention. As my partner declined to help me, I applied to my brother-in-law, William Bennett. He helped me with the necessary money, and the invention was placed in a position of safety so far as my interests were concerned.

CHAPTER X

Busy times at Bridgewater Foundry

SOON after this, the iron trade recovered from its depression. In order to make the most effective demonstration of the powers and capabilities of my steam hammer, I constructed one of 30 cwt. hammer-block, with a clear four feet range of fall. I soon had it set to work; and its energetic services helped us greatly in our smith and forge work. It was admired by all observers. People came from a distance to see it. Mechanics and iron-founders wondered at the new power which had been born. The precision and beauty of its action seemed marvellous. The attendant could, by means of the steam slide-valve lever in his hand, transmit his will to the action of the hammer, and thus *think* in blows. The machine combined great power with gentleness. The hammer could be made to give so gentle a blow as to crack the end of an egg placed in a wine-glass on the anvil; whilst the next blow would shake the parish,[1] or be instantly arrested in its descent midway.

Hand-gear was the original system introduced in working the hammer. A method of self-acting was afterwards added. In 1843, I admitted steam above the piston, to aid gravitation. This was an important improvement. The self-acting arrangement was eventually done away with, and hand-gear again became all but universal.

There was no want of orders when the valuable qualities of the steam hammer came to be seen and experienced. One of its most important uses was in forging anchors. Under the old system, anchors—upon the soundness of which the safety of ships so often depends—were forged upon the 'bit by bit' system. The various pieces of an anchor were welded together, but at the parts where the different pieces of iron were joined, flaws often occurred; the parts would break off— blades from the stock, or flukes from the blades—and leave the vessel, which relied upon the security of its anchor, at the risk of the winds and the waves. By means of the steam hammer these risks were averted. The slag was driven out during the hammering process. The anchor was sound throughout because it was welded as a whole.

Those who are technically acquainted with smith work as it used to be practised, by what I term the 'bit by bit' system— that is, of building up from many separate parts of iron, after-wards welded together into the required form—can appreciate

---

[1] This is no mere figure of speech. I have heard the tea-cups rattle in the cupboard in my house a quarter of a mile from the place where the hammer was at work. I was afterwards informed that the blows of my great steam hammer at Woolwich Arsenal were sensibly felt at Greenwich Observatory, about two miles distant.

PLATE VI

AN EARLY STEAM HAMMER AT WORK

(After a painting by James Nasmyth)

the vast practical value of the Die method brought into general use by the controllable but immense power of the steam hammer. At a very early period of my employment of the steam hammer, I introduced the system of stamping masses of welding hot iron as if it had been clay, and forcing it into suitable moulds or dies placed upon the anvil. This practice had been in use on a small scale in the Birmingham gun trade. The ironwork of firearms was thus stamped into exact form. But, until we possessed the wide range and perfectly controllable powers of the steam hammer, the stamping system was confined to comparatively small portions of forge work. The new power enabled the die and stamp system to be applied to the largest class of forge work; and another era in the working of ponderous masses of smith and forge work commenced, and has rapidly extended until the present time.

In 1840 I furnished Sir Edward Parry with a drawing of my steam hammer, in the hope that I might induce him to recommend its adoption in the Royal Dockyards. Sir Edward was at that time the head director of the steam marine of England. That was after the celebrity he had acquired through his Arctic voyages. I was of opinion that the hammer might prove exceedingly useful in forging anchors and large ironwork in those great establishments. Sir Edward appeared to be much struck with the simplicity and probable efficiency of the invention. But the Admiralty Board were very averse from introducing new methods of manufacturing into the dockyards. Accordingly, my interview with Sir Edward Parry, notwithstanding his good opinion, proved fruitless.

Time passed by. I had furnished steam hammers to the principal foundries in England. I had sent them abroad, even to Russia. At length it became known to the Lords of the Admiralty that a new power in forging had been introduced. This was in 1843, three years after I had submitted my design to

Sir Edward Parry. The result was that my Lords appointed a deputation of intelligent officers to visit my foundry at Patricroft to see the new invention. They were well able to understand the powerful agency of the steam hammer for marine forge work. I gave them every opportunity for observing its action. They were much pleased, and I may add astonished, at its range, power, and docility.

Besides showing them my own steam hammer, I took the deputation to the extensive works of Messrs Rushton and Eckersley, where they saw one of my five-ton hammer-block steam hammers in full action. It was hammering out some wrought-iron forgings of the largest class, as well as working upon smaller forgings. By exhibiting the wide range of power of the steam hammer, I entirely satisfied these gentlemen of its fitness for all classes of forgings for the naval service. They reported to the Admiralty accordingly, and in a few days we received an official letter, with an order for a steam hammer having a 50 cwt. hammer-block, together with the appropriate boiler, crane, and forge furnace, so as to equip a complete forge shop at Devonport Dockyard. This was my first order from the Government for a steam hammer.

When everything was ready, I set out for Devonport to see the hammer and the other portions of the machinery carefully erected. In about a fortnight it was ready for its first stroke. As good luck would have it, the Lords of the Admiralty were making their annual visit of inspection to the dockyard that day. They arrived too late in the afternoon for a general inspection of the establishment; but they asked the superintending admiral if there was anything of importance which they might see before the day closed. The admiral told them that the most interesting novelty in the dockyard was the starting of Nasmyth's steam hammer. 'Very well,' they said, 'let us go and see that.'

I was there, with the two mechanics I had brought with me from Patricroft to erect the steam hammer. I took share and

PLATE VII

A MODERN STEAM HAMMER

It differs very little in design from Nasmyth's original invention

(By permission, Messrs Nasmyth, Wilson & Co., Ltd., Bridgewater Foundry)

share alike in the work. The Lords were introduced to me, and I proceeded to show them the hammer. I passed it through its paces. I made it break an eggshell in a wine-glass without injuring the glass. It was as neatly effected by the two-and-a-half ton hammer as if it had been done by an egg-spoon. Then I had a great mass of white-hot iron swung out of the furnace by a crane and placed upon the anvil block. Down came the hammer on it with ponderous blows. My Lords scattered to the extremities of the workshop, for the splashes and sparks of hot metal flew about. I went on with the hurtling blows of the hammer, and kneaded the mass of iron as if it had been clay.

After finishing off the forging, my Lords gathered round the hammer again, when I explained to them the rationale of its working, and the details of its construction. They honoured me with their careful attention, and expressed their admiration at the hammer's wonderful range of power and delicacy of touch, in this new application of the force of steam.

The afternoon was a most important one for me in more ways than one, although I cannot venture to trouble my readers with the details. It was followed, however, by an order to supply all the Royal Dockyard forge departments with a complete equipment of steam hammers, and all the requisite accessories. These were supplied in due time, and gave in every case the highest satisfaction. The forgings were found to be greatly better, and almost absurdly cheaper than those done by the old ' bit by bit ' building-up process. The danger of flaws was entirely done away with; and, in the case of anchors, this was a consideration of life and death to the seamen, who depend for their safety upon the soundness of the forgings.

(Before he left Devonport, Nasmyth was asked to design a steam pile-driver, to work on the same principle as the steam hammer. Thousands of piles had to be driven into the shore at Devonport during the work of extending the Dockyard there.)

So soon as I had returned home, I set to work and prepared

the working drawings of the steam pile-drivers. They were soon completed, conveyed to Devonport, and erected on the spot where they were to be used. They were ready on the 3rd of July 1845. Some preliminary pile-driving had been done in the usual way, in order to make a stage or elevated way for my pile-driver to travel along the space where the permanent piles were to be driven. I arranged my machines so that they might travel by their own locomotive powers along the whole length of the coffer-dam, and also that they should hoist up the great logs of Baltic timber which formed the piles into their proper places before being driven. There was a great deal of curiosity in the dockyard as to the action of the new machine. The pile-driving machine-men gave me a good-natured challenge to vie with them in driving down a pile. They adopted the old method, while I adopted the new one. The resident managers sought out two great pile logs of equal size and length— 70 feet long and 18 inches square. At a given signal we started together. I let in the steam, and the hammer at once began to work. The four-ton block showered down blows at the rate of eighty a minute; and in the course of *four and a half minutes* my pile was driven down to the required depth. The men working at the ordinary machine had only begun to drive. It took them upwards of *twelve hours* to complete the driving of their pile!

Such a saving of time in the performance of similar work— by steam *versus* manual labour—had never before been witnessed. The energetic action of the steam hammer, sitting on the shoulders of the pile high up aloft, and following it suddenly down, the rapidly hammered blows keeping time with the flashing out of the waste steam at the end of each stroke, was indeed a remarkable sight. When my pile was driven, the hammer-block and guide case were speedily re-hoisted by the small engine that did all the labouring and locomotive work of the machine; the steam hammer portion of which was then

PLATE VIII

NASMYTH'S STEAM PILE-DRIVER

The only difference between this up-to-date pile-driver and the one
originally designed by Nasmyth is that in the later machine the mast
is made to slope instead of being fixed in an upright position

(*By permission, Messrs Nasmyth, Wilson & Co., Ltd., Bridgewater Foundry*)

lowered on to the shoulders of the next pile in succession. Again it set to work. At this the spectators, crowding about in boats, pronounced their approval in the usual British style of 'three cheers!' My new pile-driver was thus acknowledged as another triumphant proof of the power of steam.

The rapid extension of railways and steam navigation, both at home and abroad, occasioned a largely increased demand for machinery of all kinds. Our order-book was always full; and every mechanical workshop felt the impulse of expanding trade. There was an increased demand for skilled mechanical labour—a demand that was far in excess of the supply. Employers began to outbid each other, and wages rapidly rose. At the same time the disposition to steady exertion on the part of the workmen began to decline.

This state of affairs had its usual effect. It increased the demand for self-acting tools, by which the employers might increase the productiveness of their factories without having to resort to the costly and untrustworthy method of meeting the demand by increasing the number of their workmen. Machine tools were found to be of much greater advantage. They displaced hand-dexterity and muscular force. They were unfailing in their action. They could not possibly go wrong in planing and turning, because they were regulated by perfect self-acting arrangements. They were always ready for work, and never required a holiday or a Saint Monday.

As the Bridgewater Foundry had been so fortunate as to earn for itself a considerable reputation for mechanical contrivances, the workshops were always busy. They were crowded with machine tools in full action, and exhibited to all comers their effectiveness in the most satisfactory manner. Every facility was afforded to those who desired to see them at work; and every machine and machine tool that was turned out became in the hands of its employers the progenitor of a numerous family.

The machine tools when in action did not require a skilled workman to guide or watch them. All that was necessary to superintend them was a well-selected labourer. The self-acting machine tools already possessed the requisite ability to plane, to turn, to polish, and to execute the work when firmly placed *in situ*. The work merely required to be shifted from time to time, and carefully fixed for another action of the machine.

Besides selecting clever labourers, I made an extensive use of active handy boys to superintend the smaller class of self-acting machine tools. To do this required little exertion of muscular force, but only observant attention. The machine tools did all the working (for the thinking had been embodied in them beforehand), and they turned out all manner of geometrical forms with the utmost correctness. This sort of training educated the faculties of the lads, and trained their ideas to the perception of exactness of form, at the same time that it gave them an intimate acquaintance with the nature of the materials employed in mechanical structures. The rapidity with which they thus acquired the efficiency of thoroughly practical mechanics was surprising. As the lads grew in strength they were promoted to the higher classes of work.

From an early period of my efforts as a mechanical engineer, I had been impressed with the great advantage that would result from the employment of small high-pressure steam-engines of a simple and compact construction. These, I thought, might suit the limited means and accommodation of small factories and workshops where motive power was required. The highly satisfactory results which followed the employment of steam-engines of this class, such as I supplied shortly after beginning business in Manchester, led to a constantly increasing demand for them. They were used for hoisting in and out the weighty bales of goods from the lofty Manchester warehouses.

PLATE IX

A MODERN MACHINE SHOP IN 1930, SHOWING AUTOMATIC MACHINE-TOOLS

(By permission, Messrs W. & T. Avery, Ltd., Soho Foundry, Birmingham)

They worked the 'lifts', and also the pumps of the powerful hydraulic presses used in packing the bales.

I never lost sight of the importance of extending the use of my small steam-engine system. It was the most convenient method of applying steam power to individual machines. Formerly, the power to drive a machine was derived from a very complicated arrangement of shafting and gearing brought from a distant engine. But by my system I conveyed the power to the machine by means of a steam-pipe, which enabled the engine to which it was attached to be driven either fast or slow, or to be stopped or started just as occasion required. It might be run while all the other machines were at rest; or, in the event of a breakdown of the main engine of the factory, the small engine might still be kept going, or even assist in the repairs of the large one.

I had an opportunity of introducing my small engine system into the Government Arsenal at Woolwich. In 1847 the attention of the Board of Ordnance was directed to the inadequacy of the equipment of the workshops there. The Board did me the honour to call upon me to advise with them, and also with the heads of departments at the arsenal. I made a careful survey of all the workshops, and although the machinery was very interesting as examples of the old and primitive methods of producing war material, I found that it was better fitted for a Museum of Technical Antiquity than for practical use in these days of rapid mechanical progress. Everything was certainly far behind the arrangements which I had observed in foreign arsenals.

The immediate result of my inspection of the workshops and the processes conducted within them was that I recommended the introduction of machine tools specially adapted to economise labour, as well as to perfect the rapid production of war material. After several conferences it was arranged that a large extension of the workshop space should be provided.

In a very short time the Arsenal was provided with a noble set of light and airy workshops, giving ample accommodation for present requirements, as well as surplus space for many years to come. In order to supply steam power to each of these beautiful workshops, and for working the various machines placed within them, I reverted to my favourite system of small separate steam-engines. This was adopted, and the costly ranges of shafting that would otherwise have been necessary were entirely dispensed with.

A series of machine tools of the most improved modern construction, specially adapted for the various classes of work carried on in the Arsenal, together with improved ranges of smiths' forge hearths, blown by an air blast supplied by fans of the best construction, and a suitable supply of small hand steam hammers, completed the arrangements; and quite a new era in the forge work of the Arsenal was begun. I showed the managers and the workmen the docile powers of the steam hammer, in producing in a few minutes, by the aid of dies, many forms in wrought-iron that had heretofore occupied hours with the most skilful smiths, and that, too, in much more perfect truth and exactitude. Both masters and men were delighted with the result; and as such precise and often complex forms of wrought-iron work were frequently required by hundreds at a time for the equipment of naval gun carriages and other purposes, it was seen that the steam hammer must henceforward operate as a powerful auxiliary in the productions of the Arsenal.

CHAPTER XI

My Home Pursuits: Retirement

LET me turn for a time from the Foundry, the whirr of the self-acting tools, and the sound of the steam hammers, to my quieter pursuits at home. There I had much tranquil enjoyment in the company of my dear wife. I had many hobbies. Drawing was as familiar to me as language. Indeed, it was often my method of speaking. It has always been the way in which I have illustrated my thoughts.

But my most favourite pursuit, after my daily exertions at the Foundry, was Astronomy. I had obtained a sufficient amount of technical knowledge to construct in 1827 a small but very effective reflecting telescope of six inches diameter. Three years later I initiated Mr Maudsley into the art and mystery of making a reflecting telescope. I then made a speculum of eight inches diameter, and but for the unhappy circumstance of his death in 1831, it would have been mounted in his proposed observatory at Norwood. After I had settled down at Patricroft, I desired to possess a telescope of considerable power in order to enjoy the tranquil pleasure of surveying the heavens in their impressive grandeur at night.

As I had all the means and appliances for casting specula at the factory, I soon had the felicity of embodying all my former self-acquired skill in this fine art by producing a very perfect casting of a ten-inch diameter speculum. The alloy consisted of fifteen parts of pure tin and thirty-two parts of pure copper, with one part of arsenic. It was cast with perfect soundness, and was ground and polished by a machine which I contrived for the purpose.

I may mention that I know of no mechanical pursuit in connection with science that offers such an opportunity for practising the technical arts, as that of constructing from first to last a complete Newtonian or Gregorian Reflecting Telescope. Such an enterprise brings before the amateur a succession of the most interesting and instructive mechanical arts, and obliges the experimenter to exercise the faculty of delicate manipulation. If I were asked what course of practice was the best to instil a true taste for refined mechanical work, I should say: Set to and make for yourself from first to last a reflecting telescope with a metallic speculum. Buy nothing but the raw material, and work your way to the possession of a telescope by means of your own individual labour and skill. If you do your work with the care, intelligence, and patience that are necessary, you will find a glorious reward in the enhanced enjoyment of a night with the heavens—all the result of your own ingenuity and handiwork. It will prove a source of abundant pleasure and of infinite enjoyment for the rest of your life.

But to return to my own little work at Patricroft. I mounted my ten-inch home-made reflecting telescope, and began my survey of the heavens. Need I say with what exquisite delight the harmony of their splendour filled me. I began as a learner, and my learning grew with experience.

In my early use of the telescope I had fitted the speculum into a light square tube of deal, to which the eye-piece was attached, so as to have all the essential parts of the telescope combined together in the most simple and portable form. I had often to remove it from place to place in my small garden at the side of the Bridgewater Canal, in order to get it clear of the trees and branches which intercepted some object in the heavens which I wished to see. How eager and enthusiastic I was in those days! Sometimes I got out of bed in the clear small hours of the morning, and went down to the garden in my night-shirt. I

PLATE X

NASMYTH'S LARGE TELESCOPE

would take the telescope in my arms and plant it in some suitable spot, where I might get a peep at some special planet or star then above the horizon.

It became bruited about that a ghost was seen at Patricroft! A barge was silently gliding along the canal near midnight, when the boatman suddenly saw a figure in white. 'It moved among the trees with a coffin in its arms!' The apparition was so sudden and strange that he immediately concluded that it was a ghost. The weird sight was reported at the stations along the canal, and also at Wolverhampton, which was the boatman's headquarters. He told the people at Patricroft on his return journey what he had seen, and great was the excitement produced. The place was haunted: there was no doubt about it! After all, the rumour was founded on fact, for the ghost was merely myself in my night-shirt, and the coffin was my telescope, which I was quietly shifting from one place to another in order to get a clearer sight of the heavens at midnight.

My ambition expanded. I now resolved to construct a reflecting telescope of considerably greater power than that which I possessed. I made one of twenty inches diameter, and mounted it on a very simple plan, thus removing many of the inconveniences and even personal risks that attend the use of such instruments. It had been necessary to mount steps or ladders to get at the eye-piece, especially when the objects to be observed were at a high elevation above the horizon. I now prepared to do some special work with this instrument. In 1842 I began my systematic researches upon the Moon. I carefully and minutely scrutinised the marvellous details of its surface, a pursuit which I continued for many years, and still continue with ardour until this day.

I had been for some time contemplating the possibility of retiring altogether from business. I had got enough of the world's goods, and was willing to make way for younger men.

Some of my friends advised me to 'slack off', and not to retire entirely from Bridgewater Foundry. But to do so was not in my nature. I could not be indifferent to any concern in which I was engaged. I must give my mind and heart to it as before. I could not give half to leisure, and half to business. I therefore concluded that a final decision was necessary. Fortunately I possessed an abundant and varied stock of hobbies. I held all these in reserve to fall back upon. They would furnish me with an almost inexhaustible source of healthy employment. They might give me occupation for mind and body as long as I lived. I bethought me of the lines of Burns:

> Wi' steady aim some Fortune chase;
> Keen hope does ev'ry sinew brace;
> Thro' fair, thro' foul, they urge the race,
>   And seize the prey:
> Then cannie, in some cozie place,
>   They close the day.[1]

I had given notice to my partner[2] that it was my intention to retire from business at the end of 1856. The necessary arrangements were accordingly made for carrying on the business after my retirement. All was pleasantly and satisfactorily settled several months before I finally left; and the character and prosperity of the Bridgewater Foundry have been continued to the present day.

(*Nasmyth wrote this shortly before 1883, in which year his "Autobiography" was first published.*)

(*When he retired in 1856, he bought a house near Penshurst in Kent. He named the house 'Hammerfield', because (he says) '...of my hereditary regard for hammers—two broken hammer-shafts being the crest of our family for hundreds*

---

[1] 'Letter to James Smith', 18th verse.
[2] The 'Partner' here referred to, was my excellent friend Henry Garnett, Esq., of Wyre Side, near Lancaster. He had been my sleeping partner or 'Co.' for nearly twenty years, and the most perfect harmony always existed between us.

PLATE XI

A PART OF BRIDGEWATER FOUNDRY TO-DAY

ONE OF THE LATEST PRODUCTIONS OF THE
BRIDGEWATER FOUNDRY

(Both by permission, Messrs Nasmyth, Wilson & Co., Ltd., Bridgewater Foundry)

of years'. One may suggest that Nasmyth had an even better right than this, in view of his own career, to associate the name of his house with the hammer.)

As soon as I was in due possession of my house, I speedily transported there all my treasures—my telescopes, my home stock of tools, the instruments of my own construction, made from the very beginning of my career as a mechanic, and associated with the most interesting and active parts of my life. I lovingly treasured them, and gave them an honoured place in the workshop which I added to my residence. There they are now, and I often spend a busy and delightful hour in handling my tools. It is curious how the mere sight of such objects brings back to the memory bygone incidents and recollections. Friends long dead seem to start up while looking at them. I do not know of anything so touchingly powerful in vividly bringing back the treasured incidents and memories of one's life as the sight of such humble objects.

Behold us, then, settled down at Hammerfield for life. We had plenty to do. My workshop was fully equipped. My hobbies were there, and I could work them to my heart's content.

When James Watt retired from business towards the close of his useful and admirable life, he spoke to his friends of occupying himself with 'ingenious trifles', and of turning 'some of his idle thoughts' upon the invention of an arithmetical machine and a machine for copying sculpture. These and other useful works occupied his attention for many years.

It was the same with myself. I had good health (which Watt had not) and abundant energy. When I retired from business I was only forty-eight years old, which may be considered the prime of life. But I had plenty of hobbies, perhaps the chief of which was Astronomy. No sooner had I settled at Hammerfield than I had my telescopes brought out and mounted. The fine clear skies with which we were favoured, furnished me with abundant opportunities for the use of my instruments.

I began again my investigations on the Sun and the Moon, and made some original discoveries.

(*During the later years of his life, Nasmyth gained a considerable reputation as an astronomer, especially in connection with his study of the Moon, upon which he published a book in 1871. He formed a close friendship with the great astronomer, Sir John Herschel, who frequently visited him at Hammerfield.*)

I return to another of my hobbies. I had an earnest desire to acquire the art and mystery of practical photography. I bought the necessary apparatus, together with the chemicals; and before long I became an expert in the use of the positive and negative collodion process, including the printing from negatives, in all the details of that wonderful and delightful art.

It is time to come to an end of my Recollections. I have endeavoured to give a brief *résumé* of my life and labours. I hope they may prove interesting as well as useful to others. Thanks to a good constitution and a frame invigorated by work, I continue to lead, with my dear wife, a happy life. I still take a deep interest in mechanics, in astronomy, and in art.

Here is my brief record:

Age	Year	
—	1808.	Born 19th August.
9.	1817.	Went to the High School, Edinburgh.
13.	1821.	Attended the School of Arts.
21.	1829.	Went to London, to Maudsley's.
23.	1831.	Returned to Edinburgh, to make my engineer's tools.
26.	1834.	Went to Manchester, to begin business.
28.	1836.	Removed to Patricroft, and built the Bridgewater Foundry.
31.	1839.	Invented the Steam Hammer.
32.	1840.	Marriage.
37.	1845.	Application of the Steam Hammer to Pile-Driving.
48.	1856.	Retired from business, to enjoy the rest of my life in the active pursuit of my most favourite occupations.

And with this I end my tale.

(*James Nasmyth died in 1890.*)

GLOSSARY

AMBIDEXTER. Able to use right or left hand equally well.

BASALT. A hard dark green or brown rock.

CAMEO: INTAGLIO. (See "Die" below.) A die cut in cameo is one on which the pattern is raised, as on a coin. An intaglio die has the pattern cut into its surface. A cameo-cut die, when pressed on to soft metal, produces an intaglio impression; an intaglio-cut die produces a cameo impression. Thus intaglio-cut dies are used in presses for making coins and medals.

COFFER-DAM. A barrier erected to keep out the water while pile-driving or other engineering work is in progress in a dock, harbour or river.

CONDENSING STEAM-ENGINE. An engine which depends for its action upon the fact that in one part (the condenser) the steam is cooled and turned to water. A large bulk of steam on cooling turns to a very small bulk of water; this causes a partial vacuum in the condenser, which plays an important part in the working of the engine. In the earliest (Newcomen) steam-engines the condensing was done in the cylinders, but this had great disadvantages. James Watt's principal improvement in the steam-engine lay in the adoption of a separate condenser.

CRENELLATED. Built with battlements. The gaps in the battlements were known as "crenelles".

CRESTS AND SUPPORTERS. The crest is the symbol placed above the shield in a coat-of-arms. The supporters are the figures placed on either side of the crest.

CRUCIBLE. A melting-pot. Crucibles in which metal is to be melted are made of fire-clay or other material which will resist the very great heat of the furnace.

CUPOLA. A furnace with a rounded top, used for melting metal. The metal to be melted is placed in a crucible within the furnace.

DIE. In engineering: a hard metal block cut to a certain shape and then used in a machine to stamp or press out numbers of corresponding shapes in softer metal. The wooden stamp used to produce the pattern on a pat of butter is really a "die". (See also "Taps and Dies" below.)

GUIDE-SCREW. The long screw which runs along the bed of a screw-cutting lathe. The guide-screw is attached to the slide-rest or tool-holder, and as the screw rotates the tool moves along the work at a regular rate. Nowadays this screw is generally called the "Lead-screw".

INGOT. A block of metal as it is cast when the molten metal flows from the smelting or refining furnace. Metal to be again melted for various manufactures is usually bought and sold in ingots.

IN SITU. In its place (Latin).

LATHE. A type of machine very widely used in engineering and in many manufactures for producing circular or cylindrical objects by means of "turning". In a simple lathe the material to be turned is fixed to the spindle of the lathe and steadily rotated. The cutting tool is held against the material as it turns, reducing it to the required shape. There are to-day numberless types of lathes, some of them extremely complicated, but all based on the same principle—that of the simple lathe.

LUCIFER—"PRE-LUCIFER DAYS". The days before the use of matches as we now know them. The first matches to ignite by rubbing were invented in 1827, and were known as "Lucifers".

MURIATIC ACID. The old name for hydrochloric acid.

PIG-IRON. See page 20, Chapter III.

PITCH. The pitch of a screw is the distance, measured along the length of the screw, from any point on the thread to the corresponding point on the next turn of the same thread. Thus a screw given one complete turn moves forward (or back) a distance exactly equal to its pitch.

RATIONALE (of the proceedings, etc.). The reasons for the various things which were going on.

RIVETING. A very common and very important method of joining metals. A hole is bored through the two pieces of metal to be joined, and through this hole is passed a rod of metal (the rivet) which has a head at one end. The other end is then hammered or pressed so that it spreads out, forming a second "head", thus firmly holding the two pieces together. The plates of boilers and of steel ships are generally riveted together.

SCREW-TACKLE. A set of "taps and dies" (see below), together with the necessary "stocks" and "wrenches"—i.e. the tools for operating the taps and dies.

SLAG. The earthy impurities which are found in molten or white-hot iron. While the metal is hot the slag is molten or semi-liquid, and much of it is skimmed off the surface of the metal in the crucible or melting-pot. From blocks of white-hot iron the slag is driven out by hammering. When cool it forms a glassy mass.

SLIDE-VALVE. The mechanism used in a steam-engine to admit steam at the right moments to the cylinder, first to one and then to the other side of the piston, thus causing the piston to move to and fro.

SPECULUM. A concave mirror of polished metal, used in a reflecting telescope.

STRATUM. Layer (Latin).

TAPS AND DIES. A "Tap" in engineering is the tool by which a screw thread is cut on the inner surface of a circular hole. A "Die" is the tool by which the corresponding thread is cut on the outer surface of a rod, such as a bolt. "Die" also has another meaning in engineering (see above).

TILT HAMMER. The old type of mechanical forge-hammer, in which the hammer head was fixed at one end of a beam, the other end of which was pivoted. By means of a simple mechanism the beam was tilted to raise the head. When the beam was released the head fell, giving the required blow. (See the small sketches on the lower right-hand side of page 79.)

TRUNNIONS. The pivots which support the foundry ladle on either side and which allow it to be tilted. The name is also applied to similar supporting pivots in other mechanisms, e.g. a cannon or a large telescope.

TYBURN. The site of the well-known gallows in Middlesex where criminals were publicly executed up to the year 1783. It was near the spot where the Marble Arch in London now stands. The "ride to Tyburn" was the end of many criminals, and the phrase was used as a warning to "bad boys" by those who disapproved of their conduct.

WELDING. A method of uniting pieces of iron so that the join is not apparent. The pieces to be welded are first heated until they are "welding-hot", i.e. at white heat, almost melted, and are then hammered or pressed together.

INDEX

For EU product safety concerns, contact us at Calle de José Abascal, 56–1°,
28003 Madrid, Spain or eugpsr@cambridge.org.

www.ingramcontent.com/pod-product-compliance
Ingram Content Group UK Ltd.
Pitfield, Milton Keynes, MK11 3LW, UK
UKHW012334130625
459647UK00009B/285